The NEW WISDOM *of* BUSINESS

9 GUIDING PRINCIPLES FROM TODAY'S LEADERS

RICHARD HAASNOOT

D1297548

DEARBORN™
A **Kaplan Professional** Company

This publication is designed to provide accurate and authoritative information in regard to the subject matter covered. It is sold with the understanding that the publisher is not engaged in rendering legal, accounting, or other professional service. If legal advice or other expert assistance is required, the services of a competent professional person should be sought.

Senior Acquisitions Editor: Jean Iversen
Senior Managing Editor: Jack Kiburz
Interior Design: Lucy Jenkins
Cover Design: Scott Rattray, Rattray Design
Typesetting: the dotted i

Published by Dearborn, a Kaplan Professional Company

Printed in the United States of America

00 01 02   10 9 8 7 6 5 4 3 2 1

Library of Congress Cataloging-in-Publication Data
Haasnoot, Richard.
    The new wisdom of business : nine guiding principles from today's leaders / Richard Haasnoot.
        p.   cm.
    Includes bibliographical references.
    ISBN 0-7931-3761-6
    1. Leadership—Case studies.   2. Industrial management—Case studies.
I. Title.
HD57.7 .H333 2000
658.4′092—dc21   99-088244

Dedication

This book is dedicated to the wise teachers who
have lent a helping hand along my path.

FOREWORD

Richard has dedicated himself to shedding new light on the age-old question of the meaning of life. Every day, we compartmentalize our lives into work and play, business and pleasure, commercial and philanthropic, even secular and spiritual. The real truth, and the heart of Richard's "new wisdom," is that there is really only one all-encompassing state of human existence.

We are each a self-contained organic device that functions based on a universal, "preinstalled" spiritual operating system. Although we are unique individuals, beneath the surface we share a common spiritual heartbeat. And our success in all that we do, including business, is critically affected by how well we understand our spiritual self.

Why is *spiritual* important, especially in business? Because critical things such as leadership, vision, creativity, and passion all live in, and come out of, the human spirit.

In my own life as a father, marketing executive, corporate strategist, military pilot, and even marathon runner, I have been torn between two paradigms. I was often most comfortable when I was hard at work driving linear and somewhat limited progress. In contrast, I seemed most happy when work was flowing easily, and people were having fun creating success in leaps and bounds. Why? Because the happy, easy, big successes seemed to be largely luck, and the conventional, hard-earned, well-deserved successes seemed more repeatable.

It wasn't until Richard, whom I have known for more than 12 years, enlightened me with his new wisdom of business that

I began to really understand how and why the high road to success worked. Immediately, I was able to make more sense of my many years of experiences in life and business. With practice, I was able to consciously create the conditions under which my colleagues and I could reliably create more of the happy, easy, big successes. And now, I passionately believe that these successes are not created by luck; rather, good leadership and enlightened management foster them.

In today's digital economy, intellectual capital is becoming even more precious than money capital. Those organizations that can best inspire and empower the human spirit within their employees and associates will achieve the biggest successes the fastest and most often. And, as the portability of labor increases, driven by the same digital economy, an organization's initial record of successes may serve to drive follow-on rounds of success simply by attracting additional intellectual capital.

The New Wisdom of Business lays out the fundamental truths of the human spirit in a way that makes them immediately relevant to the way life is lived and the way business will be conducted in the new millennium.

—Scott Relf, Vice President of Marketing
Sprint PCS, Kansas City, Missouri

ACKNOWLEDGMENTS

This book would not have been possible without the wise guidance of a few gifted teachers.

Sogyal Rinpoche taught me how compassionate, wise, and joyous we can be as humans. He touched my life and his example inspires me daily to follow in his footsteps.

Paramahansa Yogananda, founder of the Self-Realization Fellowship, provides the practical and inspiring daily guidance that has opened my heart and eyes.

Djwhal Khul and Alice Bailey provided me invaluable understandings about our Universe in their many volumes of the Ageless Wisdom.

The many talented people I have been blessed to work with have taught me much over my more than 25 years in business. I am deeply grateful to them.

In this book are the stories of some of the most fascinating people I have known. When they learned about the message of this book, they willingly made themselves, friends, and associates available for interviews. Their stories taught and inspired me. The original vision for the book burns brightly because of their contributions.

Jean Iversen at Dearborn saw the potential and embraced the message of the book. Our conversations have been positive and have helped create a better presentation of the core message of the book. Thank you.

Jennifer Piemme at the Lee Shore Agency saw the potential in this book and provided invaluable help in making a great match with a publisher.

Lastly, my wife, Patricia; daughters, Tricia and Holland; and dog, Sam, have provided ongoing support and encouragement from the time of the idea's inception.

CONTENTS

9. CREATIVITY   166

INTRODUCTION

This book is a work of passion, the passion to share a message: You can be a good, caring person and be very successful in business.

The stereotype of a successful businessperson often is a hard, cold, and tough person. Unfortunately, there are plenty of businesspeople like this, and some even have famous nicknames (like "Chainsaw") that tell you a lot about them. I believe it is a myth that to be successful means to be ruthless.

This book is about a new breed of managers who lead very successful companies by following a different path. From the perspective of mystics, sages, and metaphysical leaders over the ages, this is the path of living and leading with wisdom. Although we may not be conscious of it, there is a deep inner wisdom we all share and tap into to guide our lives, an inner sense that calmly counsels us to do what is right. This sense of what is right does not counsel personal gain at the expense of others. It guides us to win-win solutions that are compassionate and caring. *The New Wisdom of Business* was inspired by that inner wisdom.

When I was listening to the radio one day, a National Public Radio program mentioned Leo Durocher's autobiography, *Nice Guys Finish Last.* It triggered a strong inner response: "No, nice guys finish first." My experience told me that you can be nice and be successful at the same time. I was a business executive at the time, and I knew I wanted to share this message in a business context.

I quickly located the stories of several successful leaders who exemplified this idea.

The vision became clear, and what followed was a labor of passion. The easy and fun part of the project was researching, interviewing, and writing. When you do what you are meant to do, the path of least resistance unfolds before you. My passion was tested when I tried to convince an agent and publisher to take on the book. It required many attempts and many rejections, none of which ever made me pause. In my heart I knew this was the right message, and it was worthy of being shared with others. My editor at Dearborn, Jean Iversen, shared this conviction.

Wisdom is something we have heard of but probably are not too clear about. Wisdom is not knowledge. It is not related to IQ. Your job or lack of a job has little to do with wisdom. Dictionaries say wisdom is knowing what is true and right. Words like *discernment, sagacity,* and *insight* are also used. Mystics tell us that wisdom is an inner quality, a deep inner knowing that we all have. Wisdom accords with metaphysical laws that govern all that happens in our world, laws that are a mystery to most of us, but accessible to all of us, too. Wise beings over the centuries have given us many books, and some have always been present on earth as teachers.

Reading and attending seminars may help stimulate our inner knowing and wisdom, but we do not need them to gain wisdom and act wisely. We merely need to develop an inner guidance system that enables us to connect with our intuition. When we have this connection, we have what we need to act wisely.

This book develops nine qualities that enable business leaders to be highly effective and successful—qualities like trust, sharing, and listening, which we know in our hearts to be powerful and true. Our inner wisdom connects us to our best creativity and expresses itself through that quiet voice in all of us, our intuition. When our actions are guided by wisdom, we feel light and positive; we have fun. We also accomplish more than we would otherwise, and with less effort.

If wisdom is this good, why aren't more of us walking its path? The good news is that more and more leaders are discovering the path of wisdom. There was no shortage of examples for this book. This book could have been twice as long and still not have exhausted the quality examples in business today. The business leaders in this book who bring the wisdom qualities to life are wonderful and talented people. They are very successful by all the traditional measures. Some are still very early in their careers and will be even more successful in the future.

As great as these people are, they are not candidates for sainthood. Those who know them best will tell you that. They will tell you that. Some even expressed reluctance to be included because they were uncomfortable being presented as role models.

To help us know each of these leaders better, people in their work life and personal life also were interviewed. Sons, pastors, lifelong friends, and others shared their perspectives. What emerges is an interesting and intriguing insight into each person. All of these people are teachers by their examples. I have learned much from them and hope their examples will help you have the courage to walk the wisdom path to success.

1

TRUST

Trust is the highest form of human motivation.
It brings out the very best in people.

· · · · ·

—Stephen R. Covey, *The Seven Habits of Highly Effective People*

Maybe the clearest understanding of how important trust is comes from having lost trust in a partner or friend. Betrayed trust produces a range of negative reactions, like hurt, withdrawal, and anger. When betrayal occurs, a relationship no longer is as full and vibrant as it once was. We experience diminished love and the loss of friendship, mutual sharing, cooperation, and fun times. Repairing trust with someone is often so difficult and emotional that we choose not to do it.

Trust is also critical in organizations. U.S. Labor Secretary Robert Reich once said, "Trust is one of the most valuable yet brittle assets in any enterprise." We have all experienced the brittle nature of trust. It takes a long time to build trust, and trust requires many experiences that confirm our expectations.

1

Yet, a single violation can result in a major loss of trust, one that is not rebuilt quickly.

Some business leaders have noted that a leading indicator of economic prosperity is social capital—the level of trust that exists and the amount of voluntary cooperation that that trust generates. These leaders find trust to be a more important indicator of prosperity than natural resources or the human capital we so highly value in the information age.

Lost Trust—An American Crisis

As important as trust is in our society, it is at a 30-year low. A 1964 national survey found that the majority of Americans trusted other people, but today two-thirds of Americans feel most people *cannot* be trusted.

What does this feel like for many workers today? They experience a deep skepticism that in their hearts they wish did not exist. In our culture there is a chasm between the actual level of trust and the level of trust most people would like to see.

The most extensive measurement of trust in American corporations is the Levering Trust Index, a measure of the level of trust in companies, developed by Robert Levering, author of *The 100 Best Companies to Work for in America*. The 100 best companies to work for have an average Trust Index score of 65 on a 100-point scale. In other words, about two-thirds of employees in America's top-rated companies feel there is a high level of trust in their companies, and about one-third feel the level is low. The companies outside of Levering's top 100 score between 20 and 50 points on the Trust Index, meaning 50 to 80 percent of employees in these companies feel the level of trust is low.

Other studies indicate that the level of trust Americans have for people in a number of professions, especially politics, law enforcement, and journalism, is low and has declined over the last 20 years.

The Major Causes of Lower Levels of Trust in Business

The crisis of low trust is a two-way street. Employees do not trust management and management does not trust its employees.

The major cause of diminished trust by employees is corporate America's massive layoffs and firings in the name of cost savings, reengineering, and restructuring. Over the past two decades, several million people have been fired so that companies could improve financial results.

Being fired usually involves some degree of surprise. The unexpected trauma eliminates employees' means of providing for their families. Even the people who are not fired experience diminished trust for management after the ordeal. The loss of trust extends beyond the company where the firing happens. Other workers know that it could happen to them, and they do not trust their management to be any more open about its plans than the management of other companies.

Acquisitions and mergers also contribute to employee mistrust. Differences between merged companies in operating systems, policies, management styles, and other cultural elements are fertile ground within which mistrust can grow.

The major reason employers do not adequately trust their employees is the "us versus them" mentality between management and workers. When employers sense that employees are not fully supportive of the company's aims or may even be working against management's objectives and interests, managers typically will not trust workers to make critical decisions or handle sensitive matters, and they often will withhold important information from their employees.

The Costs of Low Trust

When we know how important trust is, we begin to appreciate how the current lack of trust can hurt American business. Low levels of trust cause communication to shut down. When people do talk, they are not open and honest. Crippled communication quickly injures other parts of the company. Productivity is one of the first causalities. People are not happy when trust is low. When service levels drop, customers start to detect the lack of trust and relationships with customers weaken.

In his bestseller *Trust,* Francis Fukuyama studies how trust levels impact macroeconomic performance. He concludes that economies with the highest levels of trust consistently have produced the best economic results over the last 20 to 30 years. Of the G7 economies, Japan has had the highest level of trust and clearly has been the best-performing economy over recent decades.

Despite Japan's recent economic woes, it still has outperformed all other major economies over the long term by a wide margin. Also, trust is not the only factor determining economic results. For example, poor strategy and bland products (e.g., Nissan's problems) clearly cause problems.

The Power of Trust

Trust's power is everywhere. In Japan, where the level of trust within a company typically is higher than in America, trust creates a high level of morale, loyalty, and camaraderie. When these conditions exist, workers accept change more readily. When changes come, people are not suspicious that management is being arbitrary or is taking actions that are detrimental to them. All of this enables a company to make changes more quickly—a vital asset in a rapidly changing world. Over the last three decades, the Japanese have been leaders in adapting to changes in the marketplace.

The medical community is increasingly finding that the relationship between a doctor and a patient is critical to the healing process. It is very simple—when doctor/patient trust is high, patients do better. Patients who trust their doctors will be more likely to follow their instructions. Doctors who trust their patients will give them more complete information. And trust creates hope and a belief that healing will occur. Trust is positive energy. When its focus is positive, the mind is a powerful healer.

As American business struggles with trust, it is slowly discovering the costs of low trust and the power of high trust. Managers see patterns: success is usually associated with high levels of trust and many failures occur when trust is low. So some managers are taking steps to build trust. They are starting to share information—one of the biggest steps forward. Sharing information is discussed in detail later in this book.

One method for building trust is *team-building*. Maybe the most important power of teams is the building of stronger interpersonal relationships. The backbone of these stronger relationships is higher levels of trust. When teamwork is effective, it is usually because people trust each other.

Your Role—Creating Trust

Creating trust is a long-term undertaking requiring deep commitment from the beginning. Consistency of purpose is never more important than when it comes to creating trust because trust is difficult to build and easy to wreck. The principles for creating trust are simple and unequivocal.

Total honesty. There can be no partial truth-telling due to the fear that some people cannot handle the complete truth. Total honesty means that you share all there is to know 100 percent of the time. For years, companies have operated according to strict security systems—management shared only what people needed to know to do their jobs. Over time, the definition of what people need to know has become increasingly restrictive. Managers have seen only the risks of sharing too much information, not the risks of withholding information. When you adhere to the principle of total honesty, the only exception to full disclosure should be in the case of personal information that would be injurious if shared.

Compassion. Caring for others, not just emotionally, but actively, is critical to creating the foundation on which trust can grow. If you share information that may be interpreted as bad news, put the news in perspective while being 100 percent honest; instead of brutal honesty use compassionate honesty. Start down the road to finding a win-win solution so the news is not all doom and gloom. If we include them in the process constructively, workers can handle more than many of us give them credit for. They find solutions managers would never think of on their own. The power of solving tough problems together should never be overlooked. Today's bad news often becomes tomorrow's good news.

Taking the lead. Trust almost always can be stronger. Managers need to initiate the trust-building process even if workers are skeptical and resistant. Managers should signal that they want a more cooperative and trusting environment; if they don't, serious efforts may not be noticed in the first few months. On the other hand, too much weight should not be given to the signal itself. Words are cheap; only actions over an extended period are meaningful.

If you are a manager who wants to build trust in your company, do not use a paper tiger to build trust. For example, do not announce a new program via memo in the hopes the piece of paper will get the job done. It won't. And when you take the lead, recognize that you have embarked on a new direction in your life. You don't focus on building trust for six months, assume it is in place, and give it no further attention after that. You need to walk your talk every day.

Minimizing competition, maximizing cooperation. Competition within a company is fertile ground in which distrust can grow. Self-interest becomes more important than group interests. People are not inclined to openly share information with competitors who might use it against them. In highly competitive environments, competitors are not likely to extend a helping hand to each other. In a cooperative work environment, on the other hand, there is much more openness, caring, and compassion—which nurture the growth of trust.

Integrity. Integrity means not only being honest, but also keeping commitments and doing things because they are right, not because they are politically correct. Doing what is politically correct usually means delaying doing what is right when the problem can be much tougher to resolve.

Problem solving. Make it safe for others to differ with you by keeping your focus on a quest for the truth. When problems arise, search for solutions, not scapegoats.

Risk taking. Sometimes it requires a leap of faith to start creating a trusting environment. It can sound like a good idea but we have questions—how do we create trust and how do we know if our efforts are working? Many managers need to develop a new compass with which to navigate. The compass is our intuition, that quiet and calm inner voice that has the best interests of everyone in perspective.

Building Trust—Inspired by a True Story

Kelly dreaded going to the meeting. She was the leader of a team that was struggling. Their project was behind schedule and today's meeting was a critical one. As Kelly reviewed the agenda for the meeting, she stopped at the part of the meeting where John would report. The major reason they were behind was that John's projections had twice proved to be wrong. As a result, team members had lost confidence in his projections. Also, the team had taken actions that were now embarrassing and that had put them over budget for the project.

John was scheduled to give yet another projection during the meeting. Kelly reflected on how she would handle the situation. As the manufacturing member of the team, John played a critical role. If he failed to deliver on his projections this time, it was likely the new product they were working on would miss its window of opportunity with sales. She knew the other team members were angry and likely to challenge John. After the last meeting, there had been open discussion among some team members about their lack of trust in him.

Kelly decided that her first course of action was to listen closely to what John had to say in the meeting. She was sure that whatever he said would be challenged, and it was her responsibility to keep the discussion positive and constructive. On the other hand, the team needed to trust that the projections John gave them this time would work.

When the meeting started, there seemed to be tension in the room that Kelly had not seen before. The reports by other team members went well, and no one mentioned the problems with John's unreliable projections. When the time came for John to share his new projections, he was confident, unapologetic, and provided only the bottom-line information. Even though his new projections would allow the team to meet its commitment to sales, Kelly noticed some team members looking at each other with disapproving glances.

As soon as John finished his presentation, Patricia, who was a sales member of the team, pounced on John. She reminded John of his previous, unreliable projections. She also pointed out how much inconvenience and cost resulted from his poor projections. She was visibly angry and expressed her concerns that if this projection proved to be wrong, the entire team would be a failure in the eyes of senior management.

After two other team members joined the fray, Kelly knew she needed to step in. She looked at John and said, "John, I think you can see that the team's trust in your projections is low. Team members have pointed out the risk and heavy price we will pay if you are unable to deliver on these projections. What additional information and perspective can you share with us that will give your fellow team members greater confidence than currently exists?"

There was silence as all eyes turned towards John. He looked down at the table, visibly uncomfortable. After a couple of moments, he said, "These are my best projections. You can trust them."

Kelly paused for a moment, looked at John, and said, "John, that is not good enough. There's a lot riding on this. What can you share with the team that will enable all of us to trust your projections?"

John stared at the table for a few moments. The mood in the room was tense and uncomfortable. While John reflected, Kelly added, "John, I know this is uncomfortable for you. It is for all of us. We want you to succeed and for the team to succeed. To do this, we need your help. How can you help us?"

Looking at Kelly, John said, "I'm sorry that my previous projections proved to be wrong. I am personally embarrassed by my failure to deliver to the team. I thought I had fixed the problem after the first time. When it happened a second time, all of us in manufacturing rededicated ourselves to getting it right. We've worked every day for the past two weeks and have learned a great deal."

John then outlined the extensive process manufacturing had gone through to understand what had gone wrong and how to fix it. Other team members listened attentively. He was open when he acknowledged mistakes. At the conclusion of his explanation, he pointed out that manufacturing was currently on schedule to deliver on their commitments a week or more ahead of schedule.

Kelly sensed the mood in the room had changed. John's honesty and humility had touched most people in the room. A couple of team members thanked John for his openness and explanation. There seemed to be a renewed sense of confidence that the team would succeed.

Kelly met with John after the meeting and shared with him that the team could trust him more when he was forthcoming, honest, and willing to admit mistakes. When he provided details about what he had learned and would do differently, Kelly said that she could see the mood in the room shift. She underscored for John that building trust required him to deliver on the current projections and any future commitments.

Joe Mansueto—Founder and Chairman of Morningstar, a Leading Financial Services Company

A senior manager at Morningstar described his company: "For me, it is just like paradise." No, Morningstar is not located in a tropical paradise. Far from it—there is not a palm tree or a tropical ocean within hundreds of miles of the company's Chicago headquarters.

Morningstar is a financial services company that thrives in a competitive environment of much bigger companies because of the vision and leadership of its founder, Joe Mansueto. Joe empowers the people at Morningstar and trusts them to work at their full potential. Some hands-on, micromanaging leaders might find Joe's story unbelievable, but others will be inspired by his approach.

Morningstar has prospered by riding the wave of mutual fund growth. In 1989 sales exceeded $1 million; they doubled in 1990 and 1991, tripled in 1992, and doubled again in 1993, reaching $30–$35 million by 1995. In 1999 Morningstar's sales were over $50 million. Now the company is in the early stages of building its Internet-based services at www.morningstar.com. Numbers like these have put Morningstar in the top 25 percent of the Inc. 500. It is the recognized leader in its field, and when the television program *Wall Street Week* does a segment on mutual funds, Morningstar president Don Phillips is usually the guest expert.

Today, more than 400 people work full-time for Morningstar, which produces 15 publications. Its main publication now covers 1,500 mutual funds. Its other products report on American depository receipts (ADRs). Morningstar has gone beyond printed reports to add software and CD ROMs. Its success has attracted competition, most notably from Value Line, which offers a very similar product to Morningstar's main reports.

Morningstar's Chairman Joe Mansueto is described by his friends and associates, who know him well and can help us understand the company he created. Kurt Hanson, Joe's friend for over 18 years, remembers that his first impression was that he was a nice guy. Joe Sutton, Morningstar's controller, describes his job interview with the chairman: "I got a feeling from the way he answered my questions that he was going to be someone I would really like."

Joe created an environment at Morningstar where trust is a cornerstone of the culture.

People quickly and easily describe Joe as a nice person. Interestingly, when they are asked what makes him nice, they ponder for a moment before enumerating five key qualities. Many successful managers have one of these five qualities, but it is the blend and balance of all of them that leads people to conclude that "being nice" is a critical reason for Joe's success as the founder of Morningstar.

Intelligence without Ego

Don Phillips, Morningstar's president, describes Joe as "exceptionally bright." Don came to this conclusion over years of working with him, but when you first meet Joe, you are not immediately struck by how intelligent he is because he has a quiet, unassuming demeanor. As you engage him in conversation on a variety of topics, however, the extent of Joe's knowledge impresses you. He does not aggressively pursue a subject; rather, his approach is quiet and concise.

Joe has developed his quiet confidence over a lifetime of devotion to and hunger for knowledge. Throughout college, he focused on learning for learning's sake. He continues to be an avid reader. Thoreau, Rand, Einstein, Rousseau, and Tolstoy are just a few of the thinkers who have helped shape his core beliefs about the world and himself. Warren Buffett has had the most influence on his business philosophy. If Joe had opted for a science- or math-related career, his aptitude in these fields would have made him very successful.

Joe loves learning, and he also gets a thrill out of applying new insights to his world, like fixing a ham radio when he was younger or discovering how to use the latest computer technology to deliver Morningstar's products. He tests what he learns by solving practical problems, and he views life with an inquisitive eye.

Joe's very practical approach to learning distinguishes him from people who view education as a contest for grades or a project to be completed. His approach to learning produces a deep sense of inner knowing and a confidence in who he is. His is a quiet confidence that is never arrogant.

Many bright people love to feed their egos by showing how much smarter they are than other people. Not Joe. An *Inc.* article describes the experience of Rika Yoshida, a woman who interviewed with several people, including Joe, for a job as an editor at Morningstar. It was not until she had been working at Morningstar for some time that she realized Joe was the founder and chairman of the company.

Many people name a company after themselves. Not Joe. In fact, many people probably think Morningstar is Don Phillips's company, since he is the one who represents the company on television programs like *Wall Street Week*. Joe is very comfortable being the guiding light for Morningstar rather than a laser that penetrates everything in the company.

Joe Mansueto hires bright people who help stimulate him. They are not threatening to him because they represent another opportunity for him to learn. During interviews, he first seeks to find out how smart candidates are by engaging them in a wide-ranging discussion on several subjects—current events and favorite writers, for example. He then quickly moves on to determine how well candidates communicate—whether they are forthright and clear, for example. He looks for bright, motivated people and often hires those whose backgrounds do not precisely fit the job. For example, he has senior managers with degrees in anthropology, English, and history—not business, finance, economics, and statistics, which are the main focus of the company. Don, Morningstar's president, graduated with a dual major—economics and English—plus five minors.

Joe wants people who fit into the Morningstar culture so there can be harmony in the workplace. He wants employees who enjoy contributing to a team and are not angry, door-slamming kind of people. He acknowledges that finding people like this is difficult, and he ultimately relies on his gut when making hiring decisions. Most people acknowledge that he has been very successful at hiring and retaining a diverse and talented workforce and maintaining a harmonious work environment.

Surrounding himself with bright people at Morningstar enables Joe to find the best solutions through collaborative effort. While Joe is a forceful advocate for his own point of view, when others contribute new insights, he has the courage to change his mind. He leads a search for the best solution and is devoid of a need to be personally right.

There is nothing ostentatious about him. Despite his millionaire financial status, he usually buys his clothes at the Gap, and he dresses casually in slacks and a polo shirt at work. His car is not flashy or new. His home is a one-bedroom rented apartment, and his bed is a futon. Like everyone else's at Morningstar, Joe's office is a cubicle with no door—only a few people in personnel have an office with a door. Thoreau's *Walden* expresses Mansueto's feelings about material things: "A man is rich in proportion to the number of things which he can afford to let alone."

Joe clearly possesses intelligence, an attribute traditionally associated with success. Few companies without a knowledgeable and bright leader are successful. Joe is different because his intelligence does not produce the arrogance we see in many business leaders. His lack of arrogance has two important benefits. First, he is not deluded into thinking he has all the answers. This enables him to get the most from his intelligence. Second, because he does not intimidate others with his intelligence, their talent can shine forth freely. This is a powerful combination.

Good Listening Skills

Joe is also an exceptional listener. Kurt Hanson and Jeff Jarmuth (a close friend) describe going to dinner with him. The highlight of the evening is a spirited debate between Kurt and Jeff, punctuated with a few incisive comments from Joe. He listens closely to the debate, perhaps on a political or social topic, and contributes humor to an otherwise serious discussion or a substantive point that helps to turn the discussion in a new direction. While he might appear not to be deeply involved in these discussions, his comments reveal a deep understanding of the conversations' dynamics.

Don Phillips explains that Joe is a good listener even in situations where he may have a very different point of view. When present at Morningstar meetings, he usually reserves his thoughts until others have completed their presentations. For him, listening is learning, and he believes that he can make the best decision only after he has learned all he can on a subject. But while he likes to hear all sides of an issue, he is not a procrastinator. Jeff Jarmuth observes: "He really likes to focus in on something, solve it, and then be done with it."

Joe is refreshingly different from business leaders who use their positions and power to impose their views on a company. The people of Morningstar are winners because they are heard, and the company is a winner because bright people working collaboratively make good decisions.

Empowerment

Don Phillips explains that Joe was "extraordinarily hands off" from the very first day—so hands off that he did not write a word for one of their most important reports. Everyone I talked to at Morningstar echoed Don Phillips, who said that Joe "has shown a tremendous amount of respect and confidence in me."

Another frequent comment is that Joe does not look over the shoulder of people who work for him; he doesn't second-guess them and is "very supportive" of what they want to do. People who have worked in other companies before coming to Morningstar are the ones most likely to describe it as a "paradise." They have experienced different and often harsher management styles and appreciate Joe's approach. Morningstar controller Joe Sutton describes it well: "The people who have thrived the best are the people who worked elsewhere and worked in an environment that they did not like, often a closely supervised environment. They came here where they could do what they wanted to do or what they thought was best and not be second-guessed. You are allowed to take risks and go with your judgments, because you know if you are wrong, you will disappoint Joe, but your job is not in jeopardy."

Trust forms the foundation of Joe's partnership with his friend Kurt. When they graduated with their MBAs, they started a company that provided a service to radio stations. They shook hands to seal a deal involving tens of thousands of dollars—a lot of money for people of their ages. A couple of years later, when Joe left, his share of the business was worth over $100,000. Despite occasional cash crunches, he never doubted that Kurt would repay him. This experience and others led Kurt to conclude, "Joe trusts people to do what they say they are going to do" and his trust "assumes people operate with enlightened self-interest." It is true that Joe often assumes that others share his enlightened views, and if they do not initially, they will later.

When people start working at Morningstar, they quickly find how trusting its environment is. Joe encourages employees to take as much vacation as they need, and there is no minimum or maximum limit on the number of days. The same is true for the number of sick days: the employee handbook says, "Morningstar feels employees are responsible enough to decide when they need a sick day." Joe believes that if you trust people to act responsibly they will. There are occasional exceptions, of course, but Joe does not want to design policies, like a specified number of vacation days, to address the exceptions.

Joe describes his management style:

> My approach is that I want to work on a collegial basis with people. . . . My management style is certainly not the "General Patton, barking out the orders, this is how it is going to be, you will follow these marching instructions" style. . . . It is trying to get the best out of people by encouraging them and letting the ideas win out. . . . I don't want to abuse my position. I want to work as part of a turned-on team. I am a delegator. I like to give people a lot of autonomy. That is

how I would like to be treated if I had a manager. I like to give people a wide area to maneuver by giving them general goals and guidelines and let them figure out how to do it. I certainly do not want to micromanage people. I think a lot more can get done that way. I think people want room to express their own creativity and do something their way. I certainly don't have the ideas to solve all of these problems. If people are looking to me to solve all the problems, then we are both in trouble.

Most of us have had the great experience of someone trusting us and letting us do our best. Unfortunately, most managers, even those deemed to be successful, do not trust people as much as Joe does. The typical approach today is more micromanagement than trust. Some managers profess to trust their employees, but few do so to the degree that Joe does. His trust feels good, and it makes people more productive.

Positive, Steady, and Calm

Kurt first noticed Joe's ability to be calm and steady when they were roommates at the University of Chicago. Kurt describes a party they hosted that got loud and raucous at times, as dorm parties can on a weekend. While this was going on, Joe sat in his favorite chair, focusing on a good book and occasionally taking a nip of his favorite Louisiana hot sauce—a personal habit that amused his friends.

Over the 18 years Kurt has known Joe, he has "never seen him raise his voice or get angry." This is true even though both have had their differences—sometimes significant differences about how to run their joint company and about political issues, on which Joe is the more conservative of the two.

Joe's inclination is to see the positive in a situation without being indecisive or Pollyannaish. When friends criticize someone he knows, he often interjects, "But he or she is such a nice person." To be sure the discussion focuses on the total person, he purposely brings in the positives about the individual being criticized. One of his great strengths is his ability to focus discussions on a broader view of people instead of only their character flaws or skill deficits.

In the rare cases when one of his managers at Morningstar recommends letting someone go for performance reasons, Joe has a very difficult time agreeing. Again, his leadership approach focuses on the total person and on building on people's positive qualities. Some might view his reluctance to fire people as a weakness, but he deeply trusts people and believes in their potential to do well with the right help. In his view, every individual can do good things if given the chance. He recognizes that his managers are not quite as optimistic about this possibility.

Joe's positive approach to life is easily seen in his demeanor. From a distance, he appears reserved and quiet, and he is soft spoken, but up close you can sense a positive energy about him that suggests he is someone special. When you meet him, you realize that he is a person you would like to know better. There is nothing threatening about him, so it is easy for people to feel comfortable with him even in a first meeting. You don't sense that he is trying to impress you or force his views on you.

All businesses, no matter how successful, have their challenging moments. When the *Wall Street Journal* invited the company to bid on an important project, Morningstar managers did not know they were about to face their toughest moment. After all, being awarded the project would have been a major endorsement of Morningstar's services.

The *Journal* wanted to put the total rate of return of mutual funds in its daily mutual fund tables. According to Lipper, Morningstar's regular mutual fund data supplier, providing this information for the daily tables was not feasible. Don and Joe disagreed. People at Morningstar did a tremendous amount of work, including time-intensive and costly development of new technology, and made many flights from Chicago to New York for meetings to update *Journal* editors and get their input. At the last major meeting, Morningstar presented its solution and quoted the amount of money the company would charge for the service. The presentation impressed the editors, who recommended to *Journal* management that the paper contract with Morningstar.

Joe and Don returned to Chicago anticipating that all their work was about to pay off. Then early on a Friday morning, they heard that Lipper had been awarded the contract: having learned through contacts at the paper of Morningstar's progress, Lipper had agreed to provide the same service to the *Journal* at no cost. Joe, on the other hand, recognized that the service was costly to provide, and he would not offer it for free.

After all the work that had gone into the project and the encouragement Morningstar had received from *Journal* editors, the news was a shock. Joe left the office and went for a walk alone, ending up at the Taste of Chicago, a major summertime event. Don also walked to the Taste, not knowing that Joe was there, and he vividly recalls the discussion they had when they saw each other. There was no yelling or accusations. Instead, Joe "seized on all the positives of the situation," which turned out to be many.

In the end, Joe did not burn any bridges to the *Journal*. He maintained the relationship, and eventually Morningstar started providing several services to that paper. The *New York Times* and the *Chicago Tribune* ended up acquiring from Morningstar the service it had worked so hard to develop for the *Wall Street Journal*.

Joe's leadership produces a focus on the positives—the positives both in people and in apparently disappointing or problematic business situations. This is a rare strength in today's corporate environment, where there is usually intense focus on the negatives, both real and potential.

Friends are not surprised by Joe's ability to be calm and steady when adversity strikes in business. They describe him as "laid back," as a person who carefully thinks things through before speaking or taking action. This reflective quality enables him to elicit positive, supportive responses in the toughest of times.

In business today, people typically respond to adversity with intensity and seriousness, often raising their voices as if to underscore the urgency of a situation. But when people do not have to cope with an angry and threatening boss, they not only feel better, but they are also much more effective in their responses to urgent situations.

Generosity

Morningstar Controller Joe Sutton notes a core belief that seems to guide Joe's generosity toward others: "If you work hard for Joe, regardless of how much he pays you, he feels that he owes you something."

Morningstar provides comprehensive health benefits with no deductible and, consistent with Joe's love of learning, a tuition reimbursement program to encourage continuing education. Other benefits include stock options for people who have worked at Morningstar for more than two years; free snacks like fruit, Starbucks coffee, and sodas; and a six-week, paid sabbatical every four years. There are also fun events like a pumpkin carving contest for Halloween. Joe's goal is to create "a warm and cozy place to work."

His generosity is also demonstrated by his commitment to people. A few years ago, Morningstar began trying to sell its services in England. A Chicago-based manager volunteered for the project and was enthusiastic about its prospects. Morningstar learned that England, unfortunately, required a series of government approvals before Morningstar could actually sell any reports. Two years into the project, additional people went from Chicago to England to help obtain the necessary approvals. Joe's Chicago-based managers repeatedly recommended closing down the costly venture. He refused despite the increasingly persuasive arguments of his senior managers.

Again, his focus was on the potential and positives of the opportunity. Willing to go farther than his Chicago-based managers in giving people the chance to fulfill their vision, he gave his managers in England every chance to build a business that they were enthusiastic about. His loyalty to them cost him hundreds of thousands of dollars. It was not until the managers in England gave up that he agreed to close the office.

The typical approach today is to not be generous. We read of reduced or eliminated benefits and stinginess in granting wage increases. At Morningstar we see that trust and freedom translate into doing what is right for people. Not only do people feel good when they experience generosity, but they also want to reciprocate by giving their best efforts.

Excerpts from Morningstar's employee handbook reflect Joe's personality:

- Morningstar's goal is to create great products that help people make better investment decisions.
- Great means innovative products that exceed people's expectations—by a wide margin. It means products that are intuitive, intelligent, well designed, useful, and error-free.

And from the section on core values:

- First of all, we want to produce innovative products. If it has already been done, we don't want to do it. We have to find ways to add significant, distinguishing elements that set our products far above their competitors.
- People should have a consistently positive experience with Morningstar.
- Be consistent. It's not enough for a person to experience excellent service once. They must get it every time or they will think it was a fluke. Remember, a bad reputa-

tion is easy to gain and hard to lose, but a good reputation is hard to gain and easy to lose.

- Even bozos deserve the best.
- Be sincere. In order to provide great customer service, you must really want to provide great support.
- Be willing to go the extra mile. There are a lot of little things we don't have to do, but can.
- Say yes. Our standard response should be "yes, we can do that," but if for some reason we cannot honor the request, don't just say no. Try to offer something that might meet the caller's needs, even if it's not exactly what the person wants.
- Underpromise, overdeliver.
- Little things mean a lot.
- You are Morningstar.
- To create great products, we need great people.
- People who can manage themselves and their workloads, and who take initiative, can do the most for Morningstar. If you see something that can be improved, please let your manager know—or go ahead and correct it.
- The environment here should only fuel your enthusiasm and passion for what we are trying to achieve. We've tried to remove obstacles—excessive bureaucracy and narrow job descriptions, for example—that might constrict your efforts.
- Morningstar should offer a creative environment that lets people think broadly and question current practices.
- We expect everyone at Morningstar to behave with the highest ethical standards.
- If you enjoy your work, it should be fun. We owe it to ourselves to find ways to make this experience a positive one for everyone (after all, we spend most of our waking hours at work). Having fun doesn't mean spending

the day playing video games. It does mean liking what you do, approaching your work with vigor and zest, and taking pride in what you accomplish. We hope everyone shares this enthusiasm for what Morningstar is about and where the company is headed.

- A final note: It's hard to create great products if you are stressed out—so be good to yourself. Find ways to ease the tension and stress of daily work. Go out for a short walk, listen to some favorite music, take the time to eat a good meal, or do some reading in our library. Then you can approach your work with a fresh perspective and a refreshed spirit.

Its spirit and attitude of trust has made Morningstar, a relatively new company, highly successful in an industry that is very difficult to enter. In less than a decade, Morningstar has established itself as a major player in an industry long dominated by companies like Value Line and Lipper Services. Joe has created a company in which innovation and excellence are nurtured in an atmosphere of trust. His vision has enabled Morningstar to be a leader in a highly competitive industry.

Concluding Thoughts

We often take trust for granted in our relationships, or if we do think about it, we give it only a cursory examination. Maybe trust remains on the fringes of our consciousness because we fear seeing the truth of low trust. It is painful when we realize that trust is limited in any way, when we know that painful surprises may be ahead.

But when we scrutinize trust, we quickly see its critical importance. When we think about it, most of us realize how little trust we have for others. We find ourselves living in a conditional world, expecting violations of trust. Politicians, doctors, retailers, manufacturers, friends—almost everyone we can think of—do not receive our full trust.

Yet, when we experience, even briefly, a relationship in which trust is absolute and unchallenged, it is exhilarating. What power is unleashed!

This is the sense I get when I talk to Joe Mansueto and the people who know him best. A rare level of trust exists at Morningstar. It is not a perfect company, but it is a bright, shining example, so much better than the vast majority of successful companies. When we connect with the Morningstar experience, we sense the power of trust. Feeling even a small portion of that energy should be enough to inspire most of us to find a way to bring more of it into our lives.

Trust is so important. Look at your environment. Where is trust low? What can you do urgently and powerfully to move it in the direction of complete, absolute trust?

Do not be intimidated by the apparent magnitude of the challenge. Have the strongest of intentions to create complete trust, and let your intuition help you handle the details. Take unconditional actions to build trust around you. When you lead the way, you do not need other people to do anything in response. They will follow eventually. Keep the faith; keep the inspiration burning and showing the way. As you know if you connected in the slightest way with the Morningstar story, trust is worth devotion.

2

LISTENING

*It is the province of knowledge to speak, and
it is the privilege of wisdom to listen.*

· · · · ·

—Oliver Wendell Holmes

Listening is the lubrication that enables trust to work smoothly.

Listening is so important that U.S. businesses spend two-thirds of their $50 billion training budget on improving communication skills. Jeffrey Pfeffer, a Stanford business school professor, is author of *Managing with Power,* a study of how top executives use power. He concludes that listening is one of the most critical skills successful senior managers must have. It is more important than being smart, creative, or well organized.

Listening is not only an important management skill, it is a critical life skill. Researchers estimate that we spend almost 80 percent of our waking hours in some form of communication. Of that, we spend about 9 percent writing, 16 percent reading, 30 percent speaking, and 45 percent listening.

Most of us do not need to be convinced that listening is important or beneficial. But as the over $30 billion spent on improving communication skills suggests, most of us do need help in becoming better listeners.

Obstacles to Listening

Almost every study of listening concludes that we are not very good at it. Our problem is highlighted in this observation from Neale Donald Walsch's bestseller, *Conversations with God, Book 2:* "You just don't listen. And when you do listen, you don't really hear. And when you do hear, you don't believe what you are hearing. And when you do believe what you are hearing, you don't follow the instructions anyway."

From an earthly perspective, Stephen Covey observes in his long-time bestseller, *The Seven Habits of Highly Effective People,* "Most people do not listen with the intent to understand; they listen with the intent to reply. They're either speaking or preparing to speak."

Research adds some dimensions to our understanding of our listening effectiveness. It appears that the older we get, the worse listeners we become; our listening abilities decline dramatically even in our youth. In one major study, people were given a test after they listened to a story. Of first graders who took the test, 90 percent answered correctly; this dropped to 80 percent by second grade. Only 44 percent of junior high students responded correctly, and in high school the rate of effective listening dropped to a low of 28 percent. All available studies indicate that as adults we tune out or are unable to recall half to almost three-quarters of what we hear.

The causes of this low rate of effective listening are many, and they are well documented in other books and studies. I will outline some of the more prevalent causes. Our internal dialogue is a primary cause of poor listening. Even before a person speaks, we often have preconceived judgments and expectations that handicap our ability to listen. When a person speaks we tend to listen for what we expect to hear, missing much of what we did not expect. Expectations can place powerful limits on what we hear and remember.

While a person is speaking, we judge the communication process. For example, we deem the speaker uninteresting and poorly dressed, and we are suspicious that her facts are wrong. As Covey notes, we formulate a reply based on our judgments while the person is talking. Much of our internal dialogue focuses on preparing a word-for-word answer so that we are ready to jump in when there is a space to do so.

At other times, we tune a person out or feign attention, which obviously lowers our effective listening rate. Sometimes a speaker is so poorly organized in his communication that we need to allocate effort to reorganize what he is saying into an understandable form. Some spakers also create distractions, such as fidgeting, that occupy some part of the listener's attention. When we add up all of these obstacles, it is no surprise that we remember so little of what a person actually says.

All this activity happens in our head while a person speaks because we can listen at a far higher rate than people talk. Specifically, we speak at about 125 words per minute and can comprehend at 400 to 600 words per minute. We use the difference to conduct an internal dialogue while a person is talking. Unfortunately, we tend to give greater importance to our internal dialogue, greatly diminishing our recall.

Another contributing factor, and a major one according to some analysts, is that we receive virtually no training on how to listen. This is especially true when we are young and are forming many of what will become our most entrenched habits. Businesses spend billions of dollars on efforts to improve communication that is ineffective in many, if not most, cases. Often what we learn in seminars is not modeled by management or reinforced by follow-up training.

Your Role—Becoming an Effective Listener

Becoming a better listener is not easy. And feeling you should listen more effectively will not alone produce long-term change. You need to *want* to be a better listener.

For most of us, ineffective listening is an ingrained way of being. To be an effective listener, you need a strong combination of desire, perseverance, and patience—and a plan that you implement consistently every day.

Listening is much more than hearing. The communication process engages all of our senses. Researchers have found that only 10 percent of our communication comes from our words. Another 60 percent comes from body language, and 30 percent comes from sound, the tone of voice, for example. Our senses of touch, smell, and taste are involved.

There is no shortage of advice on how to listen. Some leading trainers offer the following key points:

Listening often requires breaking some long-held habits. Some of the more frequently observed habits are interrupting a speaker, providing inappropriate (often nonverbal) feedback, and agreeing to listen when we really are not prepared.

Effective listeners enter a conversation with a mind that is free of preconceived notions. Preconceived notions block or screen our listening and tend to diminish anything a person says that is inconsistent with what we already expect or believe.

Effective listeners also assume that other people are smarter than them and that listening to others is an opportunity to learn. When we are eager to listen and learn, our comprehension and retention skyrocket.

Again, becoming a better listener is not easy. It usually requires overcoming life-long habits. An excellent method of breaking these habits is to prepare in a new way the next time you know you will be in a listening situation. Arrive early and reinforce in your mind that you have no preconceived notions. Connect with a strong desire to learn from the speaker. Know that you will learn something from this conversation. The first few times you try this method, note how much more effective you are and note also how difficult it was to follow these steps. Self-awareness and commitment to this strategy will make you a much better listener. It will not happen overnight, of course, but then it took you a long time to acquire the bad habits that make you an ineffective listener today.

One of the best programs for learning listening skills is part of the Coach University curriculum for training personal coaches. Personal coaching is a profession that has emerged over the past decade and is experiencing dramatic growth. Personal coaches help people accomplish, and usually exceed, their life objectives faster and with greater joy than they could by themselves. Coaching does not replace therapy for people who are struggling with life or an area of life such as marriage. Coaches help people who are successful in life and want to be more successful.

To be successful, coaches must be excellent listeners. A coach is trained to listen for ten areas that define people and how they are doing—their values, strengths, needs, and behavior patterns, language clues, bad habits, things that are missing in their life, the strength of their personal foundation, their personal development program, and motivational factors.

A coach focuses primarily on a person's strengths and uses more strengths to help that person move forward. It is critical for a coach to assess accurately what is working in a person's life. It is equally crucial for a coach to listen closely for barriers to a person's full use of her strengths, barriers such as fear, emotional upset, fatigue, sadness, and loving crises so they can operate on adrenaline.

When listening, coaches do seven things. First, and very importantly, they are silent—outwardly and inwardly. Then a coach hears what a person is saying, both his exact words and what he is trying to say if he is struggling to express himself. Third, the coach reflects back what she thinks she is hearing on apparently important but potentially vague points. She uses phrases such as, "It sounds like . . ." and "So what you're saying is . . ."

Next the coach examines her inklings about the person's situation. By *inklings,* I mean her intuition, the subtle, quiet inner sense that often provides some of the most powerful insights. Inklings are shared for confirmation or modification. Fifth, the coach discerns the type of issues the person faces and the opportunities the person might take advantage of. Sixth, the coach requests more information, often in three areas— what happened in a particular incident, how the person is feeling about it, and what he wants.

Finally, the coach tests what she thinks she is hearing. This can involve challenging the person ("Do you really mean . . . ?") or projecting what the person desires into the future to test his understanding of where it might lead ("If this happened for you, then the consequences might be . . .").

When I took the Coach University training, the biggest change from what I had previously learned about listening involved the shift from evaluative to appreciative listening. When I listened evaluatively, I was constantly judging where a person was right and wrong. As a senior corporate executive, I might focus on what I wanted to hear and how to leverage it to further my cause. I would also be alert for those things that would hurt my cause and quickly plot a response. This listening style appeared to be effective because I could convince people to do what I wanted. But as I look back, I can see how much I was missing. I probably "won" verbal battles for the wrong reasons and missed "win-win" opportunities.

With appreciative listening, I began to soak up the total experience of what I was hearing at multiple levels. The focus shifted from judging to appreciating the qualities a person has. This was a big, wonderful shift for me. It made listening tension-free and fun. When I listen appreciatively, I go with the flow and am uplifted by revelations, even when they might appear to run counter to my previously stated positions. The quest now is for doing what's right, not for trying to be right.

Covey captures the spirit of Coach University's approach when he defines empathetic listening:

> In empathetic listening, you listen with your ears, but you also, and more importantly, listen with your eyes and with your heart. You listen for feeling, for meaning. You listen for behavior. You use your right brain as well as your left. You sense, you intuit, you feel.

A Learning Lesson—Inspired by a True Story

Patrick had been assigned to be the chief negotiator with his company with a potential chief supplier for a new line of products. Susan was the chief negotiator for the company and would have been the negotiator for this session had there not been a conflict in her schedule. Patrick had watched Susan and others negotiate in the past but had never been the chief negotiator himself. A lot was at stake for Patrick and the company. If the negotiations were not successful, his company might not make the profit they expected from the new products.

He spent a few minutes reviewing what his company needed out of the negotiations—basically it needed certain quantities at a reliable price and on a certain schedule. He ran a few scenarios through his mind about how he might try to convince the other company to agree to his terms. He knew this would be tough, since he was asking for terms that appeared to go against the policies of the other company. The more he thought about this, the more anxious he got.

About 30 minutes before the negotiating session, Susan walked into Patrick's office. Patrick greatly respected Susan's negotiating skills; when she negotiated, things always seemed to go smoothly. Susan immediately noticed the anxiety in Patrick's face. She asked Patrick how his preparation was going. Patrick spent a few minutes outlining what he was going to ask for and how he would ask for it. Susan asked if he thought of any other things that he needed to prepare for. Patrick said that he was only focused on making sure the company got what it needed.

Susan told Patrick that knowing what you need was the easy part. To prepare for any negotiating session Susan said she did two things: First, she made a list of important things she did not know about the other company, grouping together similar questions. For example, questions about a company's values and cultures often highlighted areas of common interest. She then spent considerable time thinking about how she would ask questions. She did not want it to feel like an inquisition. Instead, she wanted the people she was negotiating with to feel comfortable enough to share the information fully and completely. She used the information from their shared key insights about their needs to create win-win solutions.

After she grew comfortable with her list of questions, the second thing she did was to clear her mind of any expectations she had. Expectations limited how much she heard and learned. To do this, she spent five or ten minutes in a quiet place just before negotiating session.

This was all news to Patrick. He had only seen how smoothly Susan's negotiations went and had not seen her preparation. Patrick noticed they only had 15 minutes before the session. He asked Susan if she would spend 5 minutes with him brainstorming the important questions he would need to ask. Patrick was pleasantly surprised at how well he generated questions. He spent the remaining minutes trying to calm himself down, but with only limited success.

When Patrick saw Susan the next day, she asked how the session had gone. Patrick told her that he had found it very difficult to ask questions and listen without attempting to reply in a manipulative way. Susan told Patrick that it had taken her a long time to genuinely and deeply listen. She found that the more she listened, the more questions she thought of and the more information she collected. She said the result was a partnership with a supplier that enabled both companies to adjust quickly to changing conditions that would ultimately occur.

Jerre Stead—Chairman and CEO of Ingram Micro, America's Largest Distributor

"The ability to listen to people, understand their needs, help them articulate better what they really want to accomplish is a critical skill." This is Jerre Stead's response to the question, "What is the quality that has contributed the most to your success?"

Listening is a great strength of one of America's most successful leaders of large companies. Jerre is currently chairman and CEO of Ingram Micro, the country's largest distributor and 79th largest American company based on revenues. Ingram Micro is not a household name, but its suppliers are. For example, the company is Microsoft's single largest customer with purchases worth $1.7 billion in 1997. It is also the largest customer of Hewlett-Packard and Compaq.

As manufacturers focus more on research and marketing, they contract assembly out to a distributor, especially in the case of computers made to fill specific orders—just-in-time assembly. If you own a Compaq, IBM, Hewlett-Packard, Apple, or Acer computer, there is a good chance it was assembled at Ingram Micro's Memphis facility. After assembling the computers, Ingram Micro ships them directly to the customer, who sees no evidence of Ingram Micro's role.

Because distributors' profit margins usually are smaller than those of manufacturers, distributors require especially astute management to be successful in the long term. As the "head coach" of Ingram Micro, Jerre has the company focused on a winning formula in the dynamic technology-distribution business.

Before Jerre joined Ingram Micro, he held the following positions:

- Chairman and CEO of Legent Corp, 1995.
- Chairman and CEO of AT&T Global Information Systems (NCR) from 1993 to 1995. He turned the $220 million loss of one year to a $2 million profit the next year, increased sales per employee from 130,000 to 220,000 dollars, and improved customer satisfaction scores by 30 percent from 1993 to 1994.
- President and CEO of AT&T Global Business Communications Systems (now Lucent Technologies) from 1991 to 1993. He turned a $5 billion loss over the six years before he came into a $100 million profit, associate satisfaction increased by 55 percent, and customer satisfaction improved by 40 percent.
- Chairman, president, and CEO of Square D Corp, from 1987 to1991. In 1989, *Business Week* named Square D one of the top 25 companies for women and minorities.
- Vice president of Honeywell from 1965 to 1986.

A few years ago, the International Association of Business Communicators named Jerre Communicator of the Year.

When he speaks to college students, Jerre advises them that if they develop only one skill, it should be listening, and that they should follow that up with classes in personal interrelations. Listening is an active rather than a passive activity for Jerre. He uses a variety of approaches to start a dialogue with most people he meets, including asking people what has made them happy lately. Another approach is to ask a series of questions: "First, what can I do to help you be successful over the next two or three years? Second, what things would you do to ensure that our company would continue to grow if you were in my job? Third, if the company is limited to three priorities, what should they be?"

Another approach is getting people relaxed and talking about themselves. Dave Finley, vice president of human relations at Ingram Micro, observes, "When he goes onto a shop floor, he really gets into people by talking about them and their families. When he leaves, people feel like he really cares."

Dave notes another quality that makes Jerre a good listener: "He has an excellent sense of what you are meaning beyond the words." The ability to sense more than the literal words is the mark of an excellent listener. To do this, a person must "hear" not only the words, but also the tonality and body language of the person talking. Dave notes Jerre's firmly held expectation about listening: "He abhors it when someone interrupts someone who is speaking."

Jerre's business card says he is the "head coach" of Ingram Micro, not chairman and CEO. Being the head coach is consistent with the importance he places on listening. "To be a successful coach and leader," he explains, "you need to do four things—communicate, facilitate, motivate, and innovate. Of the four, communication is the key, and listening is crucial to communication. To listen well, you need to spend at least half of the time you are communicating with others actively listening."

To ensure that the company hires good listeners, Ingram Micro screens for listening skills during the interview process. For example, applicants undergo relationship testing. People who have been with the company for a time participate in panel interviews where a key objective is to evaluate listening skills.

People who join Ingram Micro find that listening is a key skill that is regularly modeled as well as evaluated and reinforced. Jerre has an 800 number as part of his open-door policy.

Anyone in the company can call and leave a message on any subject, 24 hours a day. He personally listens to the messages and often personally replies. In cases where he does not, a senior manager responds. He used the 800 number at other companies, and people at those companies still talk about it. Jerre also answers between 100 and 200 e-mails a day, including messages from associates who are not direct reports.

To assess how well it is doing interpersonally, Ingram Micro focuses 14 of the 72 questions on its annual worldwide evaluation on interpersonal relationships. Listening is again a key evaluated skill on the annual 360-degree review for all managers. As much as 40 percent of compensation is influenced by the results of these evaluations.

Listening receives this much attention because it has direct business benefits. One of the many times the skill helped Jerre was when he was negotiating to purchase a German company. The negotiations had gone on for some time, but he still had not established a strong connection with the CEO of the company. He knew there must be something he was missing, so when he went into his next meeting with the German CEO, he dedicated himself to pure listening. During that meeting, he heard some issues he had previously considered trivial, but that were very important to the CEO. When Jerre addressed the issues, the entire tenor of the meeting changed, and they quickly consummated the merger in a mutually beneficial manner. Since then, the relationship has continued to thrive.

Listening is a key aspect of his focus on people. He notes, "A company's only sustainable advantage is its people." In an era when many companies put strong emphasis on sustainable advantages built around patents, technology, and financial resources, he recognizes that people are at the heart of every strength a company has. Others may say the same words, but few bring the words to life as well as Jerre Stead.

He notes: "As a leader, you are dependent on others to be successful." Over the course of his career he has attracted and worked with some very talented people. He is quite proud that 24 people who have worked for him are now presidents or CEOs of other companies, "That makes me feel really good. That says we have identified great talent and have enabled them to flourish and be successful." For him, "The ultimate measure of our success is whether we have done things that help others keep getting better."

Dave Finley adds, "It is in Jerre Stead's fiber that the way you get things done best is to have a concern for people." He explains that Jerre believes that "all the competency in the world will not do you any good if you do not surround yourself with good people you depend on and then motivate. Everything he does, the first thing he thinks about is the people component."

Jerre hopes people view work as "play with a purpose." If he encounters people who say they are not having fun, he actively explores the reasons why. About a third of the time, he discovers that issues outside of work are driving their feelings. Another third of the time, he finds that people believe there are conflicting objectives. They want to do a good job, but they find themselves frustrated and unsuccessful, recipients of negative feedback from at least one direction. When this occurs, Jerre quickly resolves the conflict and produces compatible objectives. In the remaining third of the time, he finds there are personality conflicts. The solution here can take longer if the choice is to build the requisite interpersonal skills to cope with a challenging relationship. But often a quicker solution is required, especially if the situation has festered for an extended period. In those cases, Jerre will reassign the conflicting parties. Ingram Micro also has a dispute resolution system that will address issues brought forward by any person in the company.

For Jerre success started early. His grandmother, who won a teacher of the year award when she was 77 years old, taught him a very memorable and powerful lesson: "You can do anything if you want to." In school, Jerre performed very well academically.

He learned speed-reading, a skill he has continued to develop, and he earned 14 letters in four sports. And he learned another valuable lesson: "I developed a fundamental understanding that the only way you can win is if you can help others be successful as well as yourself."

Jerre started dating his wife when they were 14 years old; they were married at 18. They attended the same university, living in a trailer on the little bit of money Jerre earned working full-time. When he finished college, he went to work for Honeywell. At the tender age of 26, he was a vice president with a superstar reputation.

When he joined Ingram Micro years later, Jerre faced a number of challenging transitions. He came in while the company was being converted from a private, family-owned company to a publicly held one. The previous leader, Chip Lacey, had been very hands-on—all authority had radiated from him, and he had been involved with almost everything that went on in the company, often in great detail. A classic entrepreneur, Chip had been very successful, but he had recognized that the company needed new leadership if it was going to go to the next level.

Jerre is a different kind of leader. He helps design the plan, but gives other people the power to execute the plan. He trusts people to do what they have agreed to do. This was a major change for Ingram Micro. There is no checking on people while they are executing a plan, but Jerre is there when the results are there.

Dave Finley noted the thinking of some people when Jerre was first hired at Ingram Micro: "Some assumed since the tough guy was replaced by the nice guy that we would not perform as well. That has not been the case." It certainly has not been the case. In 1996, Ingram Micro revenues were up 38 percent, to $16.6 billion, and profits increased a dramatic 75 percent. Ingram Micro topped long-time leader Supervalu, becoming America's largest distributor.

Jerre also undertook a major effort that probably would not have been part of Chip's approach. When he joined Ingram Micro, he pressed the company to define its values. He was not concerned that the values were wrong. Rather, he wanted the company to make the values very clear and then to hold everyone accountable for working according to them. Reflecting back on the process, Dave observes, "It was a very brave act. He said, 'We are going to draw a line in the sand and say, This may not be where we are, but this is what we aspire to be and where we are going.' We expect everyone in the company to hold each person accountable to the values. If we are not being consistent with the values, call us on it."

The company developed the following statement of values:

Our Values

We commit to these values to guide our decisions and our behaviors.

Teamwork—We promote and support a diverse, yet unified, team.

Respect—We honor the rights and beliefs of our fellow associates, our customers, our shareowners, our suppliers, and our community. We treat others with the highest degree of dignity, equality, and trust.

Accountability—We accept our individual and team responsibilities, and we meet our commitments. We take responsibility for our performance in all our decisions and actions.

Integrity—We employ the highest ethical standards, demonstrating honesty and fairness in every action that we take.

Innovation—We are creative in delivering value to our fellow associates, customers, shareowners, suppliers, and community. We anticipate change and capitalize on the many opportunities that arise.

Shortly after the company agreed on the values, Jerre surprised everyone by demonstrating how deeply he believed in them. Accounting had discovered that a supplier had undercharged Ingram Micro and was not likely to discover the mistake. Jerre quickly and easily concluded that Ingram Micro should pay the supplier the price that had originally been negotiated, even though that meant spending a large amount of money.

The company also articulated its vision: We will always exceed expectations . . . with every partner, every day. And it established its mission: To maximize shareowner value by being the best distributor of technology for the world.

Another unusual aspect of Jerre's approach is that he earns no salary or bonus. Rather, he is paid with stock options, 3.4 million when he started and at least .4 million annually since. He also has purchased at least 200,000 shares. Clearly, he does well only if the company does well.

Sales and profits continue to grow. In 1998, they were up an additional 33 percent and 27 percent, respectively, from 1997.

Jerre has the qualities necessary to make a distribution company successful. To his talent for listening he adds a variety of other skills. Dave observes, "He's a very elegant and energetic person. He thinks fast, he moves fast. When you look at management competencies, he runs the table. He is a very bright guy. He has the courage of his convictions. He now has the confidence that goes with a lot of successes in life. He has had disappointments and setbacks in life and has learned from them."

As Dave concludes, Jerre's management style "is all about communication, persuasion, and getting to the hearts and minds of people."

Concluding Thoughts

Listening. Every time I reflect on it, I am dismayed at how little I do listen. And I am a person who deeply wants to listen; it is critical to my success as a coach.

There are so many dimensions to listening. I try to free myself of expectations and clamoring thoughts. I try to be a totally in the moment, totally present for the information someone is sharing with me.

The most important lesson I have learned in the last few years is to listen with my heart, not with my logical, rational mind. When I do this, I am no longer distracted by the whole effort to formulate a reply. My determination not to script a reply while someone is talking frees up so much capacity for pure listening. When I do reply, my answer comes from my heart; it is effortless and seemingly spontaneous.

I am constantly delighted and amazed by how much I learn when I listen. We have so many great teachers, if we will only let them be our teachers. When we listen with our heart, we find that we can learn the most from people we would judge to be unlikely teachers. Our logical mind tells us that our enemies and people who are very different from us can teach us nothing. When we start listening with our heart, we find that these people become our most illuminating instructors.

Jerre Stead is an inspiration. He is successful by almost every standard. He is also a very strong, focused, and intense person. He has exactly the type of personality that we usually associate with poor listening. Yet, his dedication to effective listening is clear. He knows its power.

When Jerre listens, he is much more than an open receptacle. He has primed the pump by asking questions and creating an environment where people can feel free to share their strongest thoughts. He is an active, involved listener. He knows how much he does not know and how much he can learn from others. He knows the power of listening.

I hope you connected with some of this power and are inspired to recommit yourself to becoming a better listener. There are almost unlimited resources that can help you become a better listener, but you have to start with a deep inner commitment. No amount of world-class training will move you forward if you do not have a hunger to learn from the gifts that are before you, gifts that come in all shapes, voices, and situations. When you know how many gifts are available, deeply know it, you then can embark on the joyous experience of listening, learning, and helping others with what you have learned.

3

SHARING

Tell me more about highly evolved civilizations and highly evolved beings . . . what else makes them different from us?

God: They share.

· · · · ·

—Neale Donald Walsch, *Conversations with God, Book 3*

When we have a foundation of trust and listening, we can begin sharing. If there is no trust or listening, sharing fails to happen, or what is shared is of dubious value.

Sharing—The Wisdom Connection

If I ask you, "Do you believe sharing is good and right?" you probably respond rather quickly: "Yes."

And almost as quickly, a "but" rises in your thoughts. Perhaps you think, "but not if I don't trust a person" or "but not if what I share makes me look bad." The "but . . ." that comes to mind is a protective function of our ego, not of our higher self. In all cases, the antidote to this protective response is trust.

Trust is the environment in which sharing is nurtured and the foundation upon which it flourishes.

The "yes" part of the response, I suggest, comes from our inner wisdom.

When we consult sages, mystics, and wise beings, our inner wisdom is strongly confirmed—sharing is wise. The Ageless Wisdom, a collection of 24 volumes (over 10,000 pages), is one source of wisdom. Alice Bailey, with the assistance of a great Tibetan Master, wrote about the metaphysical laws that govern our world. In a way, the Ageless Wisdom is a compendium of teachings of Jesus, Buddha, Krishna, and many wise teachers. Its scientific tone is consistent with seeing wisdom and spirituality as science. This connection was also made by quantum physicists Einstein and Bohm, who also were mystics. Its scope is breathtaking, and its insights resonate deeply with our inner wisdom.

The Ageless Wisdom describes "sharing in all reactions, of all attitudes, of all types of wisdom, of all problems and difficulties and limitations, so that they become constructive in the group sense and cease to be destructive." Please note the intent of sharing—to be "constructive." The intent behind any action is critical.

Mystics also tell us that we are seeing the beginnings of an extended period of cooperation and sharing. Sharing will become an integral part of everything we do. Its economic impact will be to bring more of the essential resources to everyone on the planet who needs them. The new economic growth cycle will be fueled by sharing, and its effect will be the emergence of goodwill among people, goodwill that will lead people to reverse the destructive behaviors that have resulted in a low quality of life for individuals and for the planet.

Paramahansa Yogananda, avatar and founder of the Self-Realization Fellowship and one of my principal teachers, confirms the wisdom of sharing. He wrote in *Where There Is Light*, "Unselfishness is the governing principle in the law of prosperity." Again, we see an economic benefit from sharing.

Similarly, Deepak Chopra emphasizes the importance of giving, a major dimension of sharing, in *The Seven Spiritual Laws of Success.* Chopra's second law on giving reinforces Paramahansa Yogananda's observation about the link between sharing and prosperity: "You must give and receive in order to keep wealth and affluence." Sharing is a form of giving; most things that can be given can also be shared.

The most important of all these wisdom reference points is our own inner wisdom. If we do not recognize the wisdom of sharing, then we will not share just because others say it is wise. If sharing does not resonate with us as wise and right, we should seek to strengthen the connection to our inner wisdom through a variety of methods—time in nature, meditation, contemplation, and study of wisdom texts, for example.

Your Role—Implementing Two Dimensions of Sharing in Business

This chapter explores two dimensions of sharing. The first is the sharing of information within a company. One of the leading approaches to sharing information in the last decade is open-book management. Another more recent approach is the concept of a learning company.

The second dimension is a company sharing its resources and profits with people and organizations outside the company. Another name for this sharing is charity, or philanthropy.

Business Sharing—Open-Book Management

Business has gone in two compatible but different directions to dramatically increase the level of sharing. The results in both cases are impressive.

The first is open-book management (OBM), which was started in the early 1980s by Jack Stack, CEO of Springfield

ReManfacturing Corporation. Articles about Stack in *Inc.* and Stack's book *The Great Game of Business* launched the concept that John Case helped along with his books *Open-Book Management* and *The Open-Book Experience.* The latter recounts numerous success stories.

The core of OBM is sharing—of real and detailed financial numbers, of accountability, and of a stake in the program's results. The sharing is done at every level of the organization, not just within top management.

Finances. There are four requirements for sharing of financial data. First, the data needs to be understandable at every level, which often requires training. The data needs to be timely—Monday morning having the previous week's data is often the target. The data needs to be specific to a relevant department or team. Finally, the data needs to be more than just historical. It needs to include future projections—forecasts and targets.

Joint accountability. Here, where everyone is responsible for their part of the enterprise.

Shared stake. Giving people a stake in the results means more than the usual pay for their time. This can involve bonuses for achieving objectives.

The results from OBM companies range from small successes to spectacular turnarounds. Following are some examples of small successes that have improved companies' bottom lines:

- Menlo Park's Crisp Publications saw its error rate in customer service and warehousing drop from above .5 percent to about .2 to .3 percent.
- The operations manager in a specialty hardware business saw on-time attendance improve by almost 85 percent.

- Physician Sales & Service chairman Patrick Kelly says OBM helped his company increase revenues by $1 billion.
- A large company like R. R. Donnelley & Sons used OBM in one of its larger divisions, enabling it to perform very favorably when compared to other divisions.
- New England Securities credits OBM with turning a $3.4 million loss in 1993 into a profit in 1994.
- Bonded Motors in Los Angeles used OBM to triple sales and create promising future growth prospects.

The "dark" side—closed-book management. OBM makes sense. People receive information that enables them to know what they can do to help the company achieve its goals, and they receive regular feedback on their results. It sure beats operating in the dark, which I experienced at a family-owned company. This company, a perfect example of closed-book management, has seen market share stagnate in its industry and innovation is low. For a company of its size, it is more of a follower of new trends than a trendsetter.

Senior management has a low level of trust of nonfamily employees. For decades, even the most senior of nonfamily managers were not provided financial data—no sales, expenses, costs, or profit data on even the smallest brands.

As a result, recommendations were made with only cost data. The only way we had to determine if the costs might be reasonable is if a similar account had previously been approved.

Not surprisingly, bold initiatives that cost considerably more than what had been approved previously were not recommended.

Over time, the company struggled. It lost market share overall, and innovation stagnated on businesses.

In this climate, I constructed surrogate profit data using some educated guesses. By attempting to demonstrate profit benefits, I added a powerful benefit to my proposals.

When I left the company, the chairman commented that I was the only marketing person who cared about profits. I replied that all marketing people were willing to commit to increasing brand profits if they had access to real data and were empowered to implement agreed-to plans. To my knowledge, nothing has changed at this company. The chairman is very talented and skilled, but he is not a strong believer in trusting employees and sharing vital information.

Business Sharing—The Learning Company

The learning company concept emerged in the early 1990s following publication of Peter Senge's *The Fifth Discipline* and *The Learning Company* by Mike Pedler, Tom Burgoyne, and Tom Boydell. Actual company experience with the concept spawned numerous magazine articles.

A learning company shares information purposely and systematically. The first of six core elements of a learning company is a commitment to continuous learning. This happens through a program of regular sharing that allows knowledge transfer and ultimately the integration of knowledge into new routines and actions.

Second, a learning company has in place processes to create, capture, and share knowledge with people who have a need to know. For many companies, this can be a new experience. Previously, learnings in one part of a company might not have been shared with other divisions who could productively use them.

A system of critical and systemic thinking is the third element. Just sharing knowledge is not enough. Someone needs to be asking tough questions—among them, "Does this apply here?" or "How can we use it?"

The fourth and fifth elements involve creating a culture that values, respects, and rewards learning, and is willing to experiment and be flexible with what it does learn. Finally, a learning company is very people focused. Sharing knowledge only works when people benefit from the process.

A company's culture, the foundation on which the learning company program grows, is critical to the success of a learning program. There needs to be in place a culture that recognizes and rewards innovation, risk taking, dialogue, and learning, and allows mistakes to occur; without this, risk taking will not occur. A company also needs to value the well-being of its employees.

Following are just some of the many examples of effective learning systems:

- The well-known Harley-Davidson turnaround included a large learning company component. CEO Rich Teerlink went so far as to establish a Harley University to underscore his commitment to sharing knowledge and effectively implementing what is learned. A culture of trust, intellectual curiosity, and openness allowed learning to flourish.
- Hewlett-Packard relies on small teams that share learnings that enable an ever-increasing flow of new products. The company's continuing success with innovative new printers and entry into the hotly competitive computer business illustrate how sharing is a key component of their success. Today, they are number one in printer market share and in the top five among computer manufacturers.
- In *The Global Learning Organization,* authors Michael Marquardt and Angus Reynolds describe General Electric's Work Out program, an employee involvement program where employees seek to resolve assigned issues by sharing information and learnings across groups and teams. The program takes place over two days without the presence of supervisors or managers. On the third day, results are shared with managers and tested.

- General Electric also has a corporate executive council that meets quarterly to share information but not financial results. Similar meetings are held at 3M, generally recognized as one of the most innovative companies; at these meetings, information on best practices within and outside the company is shared, without financial data. The process speeds the sharing of learning to other operators, where it can be used.
- The learning company philosophy has been largely responsible for major improvements at British Insulated Callendar Cable. Between 1992 and 1994, productivity increased 113 percent, market share grew from 17 to 40 percent, and absenteeism decreased by 58 percent.

These achievements are not surprising. From a macroeconomic perspective, sharing information is one of the critical factors behind Japan's economic success over the last 50 years. Since it does not have American-style antitrust laws, Japan has not constrained companies from sharing with others in the same industry. (The fact that we call the laws "anti trust" says much about the underlying attitudes that led to the passing of such laws.) In Japan, there are ministries for many major industries. At the ministry level, there is a remarkable level of information sharing. Many attribute this sharing as a crucial element in Japan's dramatic recovery from World War II that led it to become an economic superpower.

Technology plays a strong supporting role in sharing. Hardware developments have supported the rapid growth of intranets and the Internet. Software, especially e-mail and calendar programs, facilitate the rapid sharing of information. Lotus Notes, Collabra, and similar programs also play a key role in facilitating information sharing. These network-friendly applications provide a structure to organize learning for individual projects.

Sharing Resources with Others

A broader dimension of sharing is when we share a portion of our resources (or a company a share of its profits) with others in need. American individuals and companies often are very generous with their sharing, which supports so many in need.

Charitable contributions and volunteering is an important part of American culture. As a culture we need to extend our spirit of sharing to all aspects of our life. A major opportunity to advance our quality of life will follow from this sharing.

Following is a summary of the private support for some of the major charities:

Organization	1997 Contributions
Salvation Army	$1,012,403,000
American Red Cross	479,928,282
American Cancer Society	426,695,000
Catholic Charities USA	386,545,894
Second Harvest	351,376,162
YMCA of the USA	340,337,000
Habitat for Humanity International	334,737,000
Boys & Girls Clubs of America	321,757,180
American Heart Association	273,989,000
YWCA of the USA	265,352,445
Boy Scouts of America	233,230,000
Gifts in Kind International	223,871,836
Shriners Hospitals for Children	220,123,000
Campus Crusade for Christ International	212,794,000
Nature Conservancy	203,886,056

Besides sharing of money, we often share our time. Research indicates that almost 50 percent of adults volunteer an average of about four hours a week. Of all adults, the youngest tend to volunteer the least (about 40 percent of all 18–24 year olds), with people 45–54 years old tending to volunteer the most—about 55 percent of them. Women, and people with higher levels of education and higher incomes, tend to volunteer the most, predominately in religious, health, youth, and educational activities.

WRQ, whose story you are about to read, does much more than write a check. Its spirit of sharing is infectious.

The Benefits of Sharing— Inspired by a True Story

Over his years at a large private company, Larry had wondered how the company could be as successful as it was when it shared so little information. As a family-owned company, only family members were provided financial information. In Larry's job as vice president, he found it very difficult making proposals to senior family management without knowing the financial consequences.

As he was preparing for a major presentation, Larry thought he would take a new direction in his discussions about the financial consequences of his idea. He decided that he would share some assumptions about revenues and costs in an effort to show what the potential profit benefits were. When he had his estimates, he shared them with his financial counterparts to check their reasonability.

In the actual meeting, the chairman of the board looked on with some interest as Larry covered his financial assumptions. His assumptions suggested that his idea would be very profitable. The chairman gave no indication as to whether he agreed with the assumptions. He told Larry to have the vice president of finance provide him the real numbers.

At this point, Larry decided to take a risk. He discussed the challenges he had with his job when he did not have access to key financial data. He was told again this information could not be shared with him. This was the usual response every time he asked the question.

At this point, Larry took his wallet out of his pocket and put it on the table in front of the chairman. He looked the chairman squarely in the eye and said, "I will bet you my annual salary that if you provide me with financial data I could double the profits of this brand in one year."

Silence fell over the meeting room. The chairman smiled and said, "Are you sure that you want to do that?"

"Yes," Larry quickly replied.

The chairman only smiled and asked Larry to go on.

When Larry completed the meeting, he realized that he had not discussed risking his annual salary with his family. After a moment of panic, he realized the chairman had not taken him up on his offer.

Two months later, Larry gained access to considerable financial data about his brands. Within a month of receiving the data, he went before the chairman again. He outlined his recommendation on how the key brand's profits could be doubled. After considerable discussion and debate, the plans were agreed to.

Twelve months later, Larry reported to the chairman that profits had actually increased by 500 percent. The chairman was not accustomed to saying positive things, but he did smile. Larry took this as a high compliment.

When Larry left the company two years later, the chairman noted how grateful he was for Larry's efforts to increase the profitability of his businesses. Larry acknowledged it would have been difficult to do it without the financial data the chairman had agreed to provide.

In his next company, Larry led an effort to institute open-book management. When it was agreed to, everyone had access to the financial data they needed to do their jobs and to evaluate how they were doing financially. In two years, the company experienced its most rapid rate of profit growth.

Doug Walker, Cofounder and President of WRQ, a Rapidly Growing Software Company

WRQ is a fast-growing software company founded by several partners, some who have retired from the business. Doug Walker is the W in WRQ. Since they focus on the corporate market, WRQ products are not household names. But with sales of about $150 million and growing rapidly, WRQ is definitely known by its market. Part of WRQ's business focus is on the year 2000 problem for PCs, especially in networks, an overlooked part of the 2000 problem. Their customers include names like Boeing, AT&T, Motorola, 3M Corp., Federal Express, and Hewlett-Packard.

People who study companies also know of WRQ. Here is a partial list of the awards WRQ has won in the last several years:

- Arthur Andersen's International Enterprise Award for Motivating, Training, and Retaining Employees (1996)
- *Washington CEO* citation as the best medium-sized company to work for in Washington state (1993, 1997); rated in top three (1994, 1995, 1996)
- Deloitte & Touche's Washington's Fastest-Growing Technology Companies (1996, 1997)

WRQ's Doug Walker, cofounder and president, bikes to his Seattle office almost every day. Biking 20 miles round-trip in the seemingly omnipresent rain of Seattle makes a strong statement about who he is.

Doug is passionate about the outdoors. Besides biking 4,000 to 5,000 miles a year, Doug backpacks and climbs two to three times a month. He does not let rain or cold slow him down. People who have hiked with him tell stories of the exceptionally vigorous pace he sets. At WRQ, some tell the story of a time people wore "Just Say No" buttons as a response to Doug's invitations to go for an innocent-sounding little hike.

He even brought his love of climbing indoors. Once shortly after WRQ moved into their new building, he rappelled down the seven-story atrium to the wild and enthusiastic cheers of his coworkers. While Doug would not repeat this feat, it does reflect his exuberance and sense of fun.

When he is not on land, you can find him at sea in a kayak. Here too he takes the point and leads the way. If there is a choice of rough or smoother water, Doug takes the more challenging way.

Doug's passion for the outdoors is not limited to his personal recreation, intense though it may be. He shares the good fortune and profits from his business to help preserve Mother Nature's great works. One beneficiary of his sharing is the Nature Conservancy, an organization that, among other activities, purchases land to create nature preserves.

Knowing a little about the way Doug lives his passion for the outdoors, it should not be a surprise that he takes a very inclusive and innovative approach in helping the Nature Conservancy. Sure, he writes checks, attends meetings, even lends a leadership hand—but he also does much more.

He invites the people in his company to participate in actually helping the organization. For example, several years ago WRQ offered to help the Nature Conservancy in its effort to put more land into reserves.

After the Nature Conservancy gave several optional areas for possible purchase and conversion into a reserve, Doug sent a note to WRQ employees, inviting them to participate in the review process, which required the group of volunteers to visit and explore all the potential sites and make a recommendation to WRQ management. Many volunteered and worked through the review process

The group recommended WRQ purchase for the Nature Conservancy land in Washington State's Skagit River Valley, one of the largest winter feeding grounds for the bald eagle in the United States. Doug, who had purposefully not participated in the on-site reviews, readily agreed to the group's recommendation.

Childhaven is another beneficiary of Doug's and WRQ's shared abundance. This organization provides child care, support services, and education to help children aged two months to eight years and their families heal from the trauma of abuse, and to help them break its terrible cycle. It provides the courts and agencies an alternative to taking a child out of their home when abuse is present. Instead of being taken out of the home, parents use Childhaven as a day care facility.

Again, Doug takes an active, inclusive, and involved approach in WRQ's efforts to assist Childhaven. Employees are invited to get personally involved. Initially Doug had concerns about having employees dealing with abused kids, since it could be a touchy subject for some, but the response was inspiring.

Employees have turned out to help with the construction of a new playground, an extensive undertaking. Several times a year they invite the kids to WRQ for entertainment and fun. For a recent Christmas event, they issued a call for 27 volunteers to participate in a play for the kids—far more than the asked-for number responded. Company volunteers also help with the purchase of books for the kids.

Doug sets a personal example of getting involved, which is readily followed by many at WRQ. He makes his thoughts known: "I don't think people should go to a cocktail party and give money to a children's cause or for something outdoors. People need to get out and touch and feel these things." He adds, "What you really want to do is connect them to these organizations." And Doug connects by getting involved.

Doug's and the company's focus on the Nature Conservancy and Childhaven has inspired others at WRQ to assist other organizations in the area. A WRQ development manager leads an effort to help street kids in Capitol Hill, a needy area of Seattle, generating grants from WRQ and other companies. A group of WRQ workers is leading efforts to get young, interested volunteers placed on the boards of leading charities. Still another group wanted to support police efforts to buy back guns to get guns off the streets. At the time, Nerf guns were the fun rage with some at the company. They auctioned Nerf guns and donated the money to the police to use in their gun buy-back efforts.

At times, the company's civic involvement has assisted in making a sale. For example, in setting up a partnership with a large East Coast company, it helped that both were deeply involved in the Nature Conservancy. When negotiating to do business with a large pharmaceutical company, their similar efforts to help children were noted by a key decision maker at the company as a reason WRQ made the sale.

This extensive community involvement has benefits in attracting top talent to the company. Doug notes, "Our reputation for community involvement is a very big reason a person is willing to leave a company to join us." Key people have noted the company's dedication to community sharing and service as a reason for joining WRQ. In an industry where attracting top talent is critical to success, this is a major benefit for the company.

When you learn that their turnover rate is consistently about 10 percent—less than half the industry average—you start to sense that WRQ is a special company. There are several values that Doug and the other founders have brought that are reflected throughout the company.

When they founded the company they had a vision. "We just thought it had to be possible to create a corporate culture based on respect, trust and teamwork, and we wanted to get together an egalitarian group of people that liked to solve software problems," says Doug.

Respect and *trust* are key words for Doug, and they guide how he manages. Doug sees respect as a governor that defines the quality of relationships within the company. When collaboration is working, respect is working in the background. Collaboration intrinsically involves open, constructive sharing. In the software business, this sharing is critical to developing quality products in a short period.

He also sees it impact on relationships with customers. Their customer service group respects the customer problems, which is critical when professionals are working with other professionals.

WRQ has a relatively flat organizational structure and a highly empowered workforce. While *empowerment* is often misunderstood and overused, it is alive and well at WRQ. As one employee noted, "This is a place where if you see a need, you just do it. You can take the initiative. There are no quotas, no set instructions, no one breathing down your neck."

Doug prides himself on having as few rules as necessary. As he puts it, "We use a system here that is principle based instead of rules based." Using principles instead of rules can create differences based on varying interpretations of a principle. Again, respect and trust help guide them through this process.

The key to making this approach work is in hiring the right people. The typical candidate goes through about 15 hours of interviews usually conducted by teams. While this process can seem to hinder a rapidly growing company that needs to hire people fast to meet expanding needs, it is critical to getting the right person that can work in their system.

When a person joins WRQ, he or she finds a participative management, reflected in such flexible work practices as compressed workweeks, flex hours, telecommuting, and part-time schedules. In their main office, there is a room where new mothers can feed their babies, and a room where a person can "crash" if he or she is working long hours. Of course, there is a bike storage room, massage room, and locker area for changing. A Seattle recruiter observes, "WRQ has carved a niche as a place to work where family life and personal life are very important."

What kind of person has created all this? Besides his passion for the outdoors and sharing, Doug has several qualities that make him the unique and inspired person he is. First, he is smart. Graduating *magna cum laude* in math from Vanderbilt University is only part of the story. Friends report he has a photographic memory, especially when it comes to one of his other passions—history. People who have engaged him in a discussion of the Civil War are impressed by his incredibly detailed knowledge of key battles.

But intelligence without people skills does not make for good leadership. Doug has great interpersonal skills. A friend discusses his demeanor: "He has a Southern, aw-shucks, low-key style that kind of hides the fact of who he really is. He dresses in a very unpretentious way. He comes across as a very comfortable guy who listens well and talks softly. People do not feel defensive or intimidated around him. And yet, he finds ways to elicit information and achieve his communication goals without appearing to drive the conversation." Another friend notes his "boyish enthusiasm about life" and that he has a "smile you can get comfortable with and a twinkle in his eye." The same friend notes, "He looks at the world much wider than most people do."

It is this last quality that may serve Doug best. His passions reflect this wider view—mountain climbing, a technical business, Civil War history, and sharing his abundance with others. This wider view is inclusive and is the inner guidance system that enables him to achieve his own kind of enlightened success.

Concluding Thoughts

Sharing has so many powerful dimensions. We have seen some of them in this chapter.

For me, the most powerful dimension of sharing is the one that leads to service. We become committed to sharing whatever we have to help others. This is the powerful example of people like Jesus and the Buddha from a couple of millennia ago to Mother Teresa and the Dalai Lama in the current century.

When we realize the ultimate sharing is serving others, we also realize a level of joy and love that is unimaginable when our posture is serving our needs. For someone who has not had a glimmer of the experience of truly and completely serving others, the previous sentence is incomprehensible. For someone who has seen the light, they are usually inspired to take more steps along the path.

Doug's example is a special one. Almost all companies support some charitable causes, but very few do it like Doug does. His invitation to employees of WRQ to become deeply involved brings company assistance to a new level. The level is well beyond the writing of checks. When we give of ourselves, the contribution increases immeasurably. When we share our time, we give ideas, inspiration, and concrete, practical assistance that exceeds any estimate of its value.

Doug lives his dedication to helping the environment. When most senior business leaders are trying to determine which luxury, low-mileage car to buy, Doug maintains his dedication to living his passionate love of nature and a healthy, strong environment.

This commitment and its integration into his life inspire me. We may not share his passion of exactly what we want to help with, but we can live our inspiration to help. Doug is showing the way we can share of ourselves at new levels.

COOPERATION

> • *Assume that everyone can enjoy good teamwork, friendship, good group spirit, good group homonomy, good belongingness, and group love.*

> • *Enlightened economics must assume goodwill among all members of the organization rather than rivalry or jealousy.*

> • • • • •

> —Two of Abraham Maslow's keys to enlightened management, *Maslow on Management*

When trust, listening, and sharing are present, the conditions are right for cooperation. The building blocks of trust, listening, and sharing, if solidly in place, set the stage for the full power of cooperation to emerge. Cooperation, as we shall see, is an exceptionally powerful driver of success.

Groups that cooperate do better than groups that do not cooperate. This applies to any objective an organization wants from a group. If the group's purpose is to implement an agreed-to plan, the cooperative group is much more likely to deliver on time and under budget than a similarly talented group that does not cooperate well.

There are degrees of cooperation. Certainly the more cooperation, the better the results, but it is not an entirely linear relationship. There comes a point where a high level of cooperation, fueled by strong trust, sharing, and listening, propels a group to very high levels of performance.

Creativity is the first sign of a highly cooperative group. New ideas spring forth, and they are embraced and built upon by group members. The new ideas enable the group to surpass their objectives and to create an inspiring environment. The benefits of this can last well beyond the life of the group.

Cooperate, Don't Compete

This chapter asks that you open your mind, even a little, to the possibility of replacing competition, everywhere it exists, with cooperation.

Making the request is easy, but opening the mind to this possibility is not so easy. In our culture, competing is a virtue. For most people, it is a given that competition is best for the individual and society.

For most people, the suggestion that cooperation replace competition throughout our life is a revolutionary one. In the space of one chapter, there is only enough space to stimulate and even provoke you into contemplating an idea that until now has been considered un-American, among other things.

There are books that illustrate the serious shortcomings of competition: Alfie Kohn's *No Contest, The Case against Competition: Why We Lose in Our Race to Win,* for example. And some day I will finish my book on why cooperation beats competition. Until then, I hope this brief discussion opens a possibility that did not exist previously.

As a starting point, do not try to make a decision to accept or reject cooperation as a replacement for competition. Instead, consider the case for cooperation and eliminate the need to make a judgment at this point.

Why should we switch from competition to cooperation? Here are a few reasons to consider:

- We are not happy. Anxiety and dissatisfaction are at all-time high levels by most measures.
- We are wasteful. Competition creates duplication of efforts between competing companies.
- We are not achieving optimal product quality. Competition limits creativity and risk taking.

The list could go on, but it also could end with the first reason. We are not happy because Americans sense there is something more—that we are missing something. As a nation, we have great material wealth, yet we know there is more and it may not include just more and more material wealth.

On a personal level, many of us have acquired varying amounts of material wealth, which at best, helped us to be happy for a short period until we began wondering what was next. We see rich people committing suicide and spending huge sums on therapy. Greater material wealth does not appear to be the answer.

Our sense that there is a better path is a deep internal feeling. There is a nagging, gnawing sense that the current way is not right. But what is the answer?

To find the answer, we need to look in a different direction.

For many people, spirituality is the answer. This well-placed interest ultimately will lead us to a much happier place, by encouraging us to reach out (to cooperate), as well as to explore our inner resources.

Cooperation creates goodwill, and as such is an expression of our spirituality. It brings people together in a positive and supportive way. We need only consult our heart to confirm the wisdom of cooperation. Every area of human activity today can benefit from cooperation. It is the hope of the future.

Benjamin Creme, a current Ageless Wisdom scholar, adds, "Co-operation is another word for unity. Unity and co-operation are the springboards to the future and the guarantee of achievement for all men. Great reservoirs of power lie untapped within humanity waiting for the magic of co-operation to unleash." He goes on to add a point that is made throughout this chapter, "There is no such thing as 'healthy competition'. There is either co-operation or competition. Co-operation is pro-life, pro-evolution, and competition is the very reverse. It is the opposite of life; it is against evolution."

Cooperation is an international theme. The benefits of cooperation are evident between two people and among two billion people. We have seen some indications of increased cooperation on an international level. We see it when only two groups learn to cooperate more, Palestinians and Israelis, for example, or many nations, a stronger United Nations peacekeeping effort, for example.

Before detailing the case for cooperation, here are a few words on what is not being recommended. Cooperation is not an economy of monopolies, as we know them today, and it is not communism.

For cooperation to be a powerful economic force, there needs to be an associated personal transformation. The transformation is a spiritual one where we recognize our oneness, an all-pervading energy (God, for some), and the rightness of service to others. When this transformation occurs, the stagnant, insensitive, and bureaucratic nature of monopolies will not occur. Personal transformation creates an attitude of compassion and helpfulness that does not exist broadly today.

Thus, as you consider the case for cooperation, remember that the transition to a cooperatively based system is in conjunction with the personal transformation just discussed. In fact, the personal part leads the change; without it, the vision of cooperation will not occur.

Your Role—Believing in the Power of Cooperation

Today we frequently bow in homage to the power and benefits of competition. Despite its revered status, business is already sensing the value of cooperation. Daily there are announcements of new alliances between businesses. These alliances are usually intended to help two or more companies achieve more than they can by going it alone.

Business recognizes that cooperation is good business. Neither our culture nor we fully appreciate the benefits of cooperation. While there are strong and clear economic benefits from cooperation, the benefits go far beyond direct impact on the bottom line. The positive human impact of cooperation spawns higher levels of creativity and innovation as well as a strong focus on the long-term ramifications of our actions. The concept of win-win made so popular by Covey in his *The Seven Habits of Highly Effective People* will eventually be extended to creating win-win solutions for companies, groups of companies, and finally an entire economy.

That promise walks us out into the future. The first order of business is recognizing that today's extensive system of myths have grown up around our competitively based way of life. They need to be dispelled before you can fully embrace the power and benefits of cooperation.

The Myths of Competition

Supporters of competition cite several reasons why it is superior to other systems. On close examination, these reasons turn out to be myths.

Myth #1: Being Competitive Is a Part of Being Human and Is Unavoidable

Science is very clear on this—whether a society is competitive or not depends on the values taught in that culture. Humans are not automatically and innately competitive. Margaret Mead's trailblazing work showed there are cultures with and without competition. Among humans, Mead concluded, in *Cooperation and Competition among Primitive Peoples,* ". . . the most basic conclusion which comes out of this research [is] that competitive and cooperative behavior on the part of individual members of a society is fundamentally conditioned by the total social emphasis of that society . . ." Thus, we have a choice as a culture—cooperation or competition.

The scientific evidence following her discoveries is clear and strong—competition is not instinctive. The myth has its roots in Darwin's survival of the fittest work. Study of the animal kingdom, from which Darwin drew most of his observations, concludes that there are high levels of cooperation, much of it very sophisticated. Competition usually produces some level of aggression, which is not necessary for survival and in many cases may actually threaten survival of all competing members.

In cooperative cultures, Mead found power over people is not important, status is of limited or no importance, and there is a high degree of security for the individual. In competitive cultures, property is for individuals, the individual is more important than the group, and there is a single scale to measure success, on which usually winners are the only ones seen as successes.

There are numerous cultures where competition does not exist. We consider many of these cultures as primitive, but we can learn something from these so-called "primitive" cultures.

While they are primitive in economic terms, these cultures are some of the happiest cultures, according to scientists.

In cooperative societies, people are generous with their possessions. Personal gain is not important—group gain is. Hospital-
ity is high and there are often sanctions against greed and
selfishness. Economics are far less important than they are in
most Western cultures.

And we call this "primitive"? In terms of human interaction, it sounds enlightened to me.

Myth #2: Competition Motivates Us to Do Our Best

Competition does not produce better results than cooperation. Study after study has shown the reverse to be true.

One leading critic of competition commented, ". . . *Do we
perform better when we are trying to beat others than when we are working with them or alone?* . . . the evidence is so overwhelmingly
clear and consistent that the answer to this question is *almost
never.* Superior performance not only does not require competition; it usually seems to *require* its absence."

A 1981 review of many studies done between 1924 and
1980 showed 65 concluding cooperation beat competition, 36
with no difference, and 8 where competition beat cooperation.
The strength of cooperation seems to be especially true where
quality is more important than speed or quantity.

One reason competition produces worse results so many
times is because of where we focus. In competition, the focus is
on beating others. In cooperation, we focus on doing our best.

This is a powerful thought. Competition is not about objective excellence; it is about winning at the expense of another individual or group. Think about the times you have
competed. The plan for winning usually involves at least one
eye on the opponent—his or her strengths, weaknesses, and
plans to attack you. The plan is to overcome their strengths by
attacking their weaknesses with your strengths. The objective is
not to do the best in the absolute.

The objective is to win, not to do what is right. Lawyers may be the best example of where the objective is to win rather than do what is right. Many people who have been even remotely close to the legal process come away with a sick feeling about how facts are distorted in an all-out effort to win. The drive to win overwhelms completely, in many cases, the drive to do what is right. Legal scholars and others have written extensively on this issue.

Myth #3: Competition Is Fun

When you watch teams compete, do they look like they are having fun? Unfortunately, from the elementary school level to the professional level, people involved in a competitive game often do not look as if they are having fun. It looks like work, hard work.

At work is there much fun? Again, work is a serious undertaking, where the focus is on concerns about winning, which creates stress and pressure. Only the lucky few describe work as fun, and even then it is often only some of the time.

In competition, winners are rewarded and losers are rejected. Children learn early on to compete at school for grades, advancement, and ultimately admission to the school of their choice, and not for the thrill of understanding their world better. The focus is on victory, sometimes over a friend or associate and other times over a faceless other person. This may be fleeting fun for the victor, but they quickly discover the need to win again soon.

Philosopher Betrand Russell also saw the grimness of competition.

> Competition considered as the main thing in life is too grim, too tenacious, too much a matter of taut muscles and intent will, to make a possible basis for life for more than one or two generations at most. After that length of

time it must produce nervous fatigue, various phenomena of escape, a pursuit of pleasure as tense and as difficult as work. . . .

He went on to comment on the effects of competition on leisure time, "It is not only work that is poisoned by the philosophy of competition; leisure is poisoned just as much."

While the act of competing is seldom fun, winning can be fun. Unfortunately, there are many more losers than winners in most forms of competition. For example, in the National Football League ultimately 29 of the 30 teams eventually go home losers at the end of a season. And the members of the winning team often find the moments of fun fleeting, since a new season or a new business initiative is soon upon them. Then the grim task of competing begins all over again.

Myth #4: Competition Builds Character and Self-Confidence

There is no doubt that competition does build character, but what kind?

Success in a competitive world requires some degree of aggression. Videos on the hardest, meanest hits celebrate the aggressiveness in sports. Business rewards aggressiveness and timidity is quickly eliminated. Aggressiveness in business can mean qualities like not taking no for an answer, ramming a proposal through against all odds (and without consideration of the human costs), and being outspoken. Much of this aggressive behavior is dehumanizing, because there is a lack of concern for the feelings of another person. A humanizing action on the other hand is kind, compassionate, helpful, and loving, which cooperation engenders.

A 1971 study among 12-year-old boys found that when gains can only be made at the expense of another group, the groups become hostile towards each other, even when they started as friendly and well-adjusted individuals. This is the nature of most competition. An "us versus them" attitude develops in competition that results in aggressive actions to defeat "them."

Maybe the most telling indictment about the character that results from a strongly competitive society is the broad-scale illegal aggression that results. The United States has one of the highest violent crime levels of any major country. Consider these facts:

- For the first time in our history, in 1994 there were over one million men and women in state and federal prisons, which typically hold convicted felons. When locally operated jails are included, over one and a half million people were in prison in 1994—another record.
- Over a million people in America each year face an armed assailant with a handgun. Each year there are over four million reported murders, rapes, robberies, and aggravated assaults, and more than a quarter of them involved a gun.
- The Council on Crime in America, headed by a former Attorney General and Drug Czar, reported that crime levels in America are five to six times higher than actually reported.

Our competitive culture teaches aggression at an early age, usually in sports, and reinforces it when we work in business, government, and most other fields. Common sense also says that if you learn aggressive, even violent behavior in competitive sports, you will be more likely to be aggressive outside the sporting event.

Scientific studies have found that competition in sports heightens aggressive behavior throughout a person's life. A study in *Psychology Today* (Oct. 1971) titled "Sport: If You Want to Build Character, Try Something Else" reported on a personality profile administered to 15,000 athletes that revealed a low interest in getting assistance from others, a low need to care for others, and a limited interest in being affiliated with other people.

Also, since competition produces as many or more losers than winners, it seriously undermines self-confidence. With cooperation, there are no losers.

Cooperation feels right and builds self-esteem because openness and trust allow everyone to contribute. Self-esteem is one of the most critical components of a psychologically healthy person. It is also an important factor in concluding how happy and successful we feel.

From this evidence and much more not detailed here, it is easy to conclude that we can do a better job of building character than our competitive system produces.

Myth #5: Competition Results in Lower Prices

With the right individual spirit, cooperation will produce the most significant price reductions in our history. Price decreases of 30 to 50 percent in conjunction with improved product performance are reasonable to expect.

A competitive economy involves tremendous redundancy. Any product could be an example, but the bar soap business illustrates the point. There are five major companies selling bar and liquid soaps today—Procter & Gamble (Ivory, Zest, Safeguard, Camay, Lava, Oil of Olay), Lever Brothers (Dove, Shield, Caress, Lever 2000), Colgate-Palmolive (Irish Spring, Palmolive), Dial, and Jergens, plus some smaller companies and private label manufacturers.

All these companies have finance, sales, marketing, production, and research dedicated directly to these products, and also support functions like legal and creative design, where part of the function works on bar soaps. In each company, there are probably hundreds of people performing these functions. The actual cost of ingredients and manufacturing composes about 50 percent of the company's selling cost, with the other 50 percent going to pay for the duplicated costs and a profit.

From a consumer standpoint, there is no benefit to paying for five sales organizations, five marketing groups, and five finance groups. Consumer research is done five times, most of the same questions are asked, and the answers are largely the same. All this does is produce higher costs for consumers than a cooperative approach would. If one company manufactured and distributed bar soaps, prices could be dramatically lower.

The same is roughly true for many other consumer and industrial products.

For many people, this myth may be the hardest to dispel. For years, most of us have been brought up to believe that competition creates lower prices. The thinking goes that without the threat of a competitor taking a company's business that they would raise their prices endlessly. In today's culture that rewards material accumulation and bestows status to those who make more money, this view is very understandable.

Without going too far out, the wisdom traditions of all cultures of all times remind us that materialism is not the wisest of paths. As we embrace these wisdom traditions, we will become more dedicated to helping and serving others in ways that already can be seen. The most visible manifestation is the current spiritual awakening. Its messages of compassion and unity are the foundation on which cooperation will grow. When fully developed, a cooperative economy will provide lower prices through cooperation and resist the power of person or collective greed that propels today's seemingly insatiable quest for money and material possessions.

Myth #6: Competition Leads to Greater Innovation

Take a look at the products we use the most—those bought in a grocery store. Very little true innovation has been made in these categories over the last 10 to 20 years. Soaps still clean, paper towels still clean up, tomato soup tastes like tomatoes, and Pepsi still tastes sweeter than Coke.

Manufacturers try to differentiate their products through image and differences that are not real or meaningful. Consider the example of two deodorant products, Sure and Secret, both from Procter & Gamble. The ingredients are the same, and with slight perfume differences, they *are* the same. Yet, Secret claims to be pH-balanced for a woman; but Sure has the same pH. Consumers may pay extra for a deodorant soap that claims to kill germs, but Ivory, one of the simplest and most basic soaps, kills the same number of germs and costs a lot less. The same principle applies to most products in the grocery store.

But what about technology? There has been some true innovation there, but is it innovation that would not have happened with a cooperative system?

Personal computers are pretty much the same. Product reviews in trade publications reveal only slight differences among computers run by the same processor. The main processors are the same, the motherboards are often from the same supplier or are very similar, and there are small differences in the add-on boards in the computers. There may be some noticeable differences, if you look at the extremes in a 20-company review, but for the most part the differences are more technical and statistical than user-noticeable.

When innovation does occur, the manufacturer's instinct in today's competitive system is to charge the consumer a premium far beyond the actual cost. These companies figure they are the only ones with the feature; therefore, consumers will pay more. Apple did this with computers for a long time.

In a cooperative system, consumers would expect to pay the actual cost premium and no more. Because talent and resources are pooled in a cooperative system, innovation occurs faster and at a lower cost.

Think of the knowledge that individual companies have that, if shared, would lead to joining all the missing pieces of the puzzle. The research business, especially the disease research area, is becoming more and more competitive. Scientists are hoping for individual glory, as Jonas Salk achieved for curing polio. This motivation limits the sharing of research findings in such areas as the search for a cure for AIDS. We can only wonder about how fast we could move if there were cooperation with complete and open sharing among all the research groups. This could happen if competition could be replaced with a truly cooperative system and culture.

The benefits become even more powerful when all industries share their knowledge, since the technology in one industry can benefit companies in other businesses. One of the highest potential areas is the sharing of technology, especially technology classified as secret or top secret by the government. In addition, the sharing of patented technology eventually will allow the combining of technologies that cannot occur today.

We already see signs of sharing of technology in America, with companies broadly licensing their patents to other companies. While most of these are not directly competing companies, there some licensing agreements exist between some bitter competitors. For example, Sun licensed Java, a programming system, to its rival in many markets, Microsoft. At this time, all licensing of technology is done with self-interest being paramount. The time is coming when the motivation will be more to aid all of humanity. That is the wiser way.

Cooperation Today

As a society we do not have much experience with cooperation. Business has adopted the team process, for example, but these teams still operate in a competitive system.

Having said this, the trend does seem to be moving toward more cooperation. Most days we read announcements of many new alliances between companies. Teams are truly well established in most companies. Serious efforts have been made to break down barriers between functions and divisions. Compensation rewards group results. But we need to be clear that all this progress is happening within a competitive macroeconomy.

We can get some helpful insights on cooperation from scientists who have developed game theories. Not surprisingly, with current attitudes and beliefs, reciprocity plays a significant role in their findings.

Unfortunately, to learn about the full benefits of cooperation in the United States, it had to be studied in a somewhat laboratory-like environment. Increasingly, scholars and business leaders are noting the costs of low or nonexistent cooperation—inhibited innovation, less than satisfactory customer service, low product quality, and wasted resources.

Scientists have found that cooperation may emerge for negative reasons—a fear of retribution. In these cases, it may look like cooperation but it almost always is a tempered competition. Since people know they will meet again and need to work together, they temper their competitive and aggressive tendencies.

A natural next step in this approach to cooperation is being nice to others; for example, being compassionate and a good listener. Being nice can be infectious and enjoyable. This enjoyment often then leads to more wholehearted cooperation. Cooperation is fun, even joyful. When people experience this benefit of cooperation, they become enthusiastic proponents of cooperation.

When true cooperation is in place, there is usually a common purpose, coordination, and meeting of diverse needs, and people fully leverage their skills. Cooperative goals address the needs of many, while competition focuses more on individual needs.

Your Role—Building
Cooperation One Step at a Time

We have already seen the building blocks of cooperation—trust, sharing, and listening. If any one of these is not valued in an organization, the full benefits of cooperation will not emerge.

When these values are fully a part of an organization's culture, the systems and structures need to change to fully support the emergence of cooperation. The formation of ongoing and short-lived teams often signals the breaking apart of "silo" management, which fosters the parochial, narrow interests of functions and divisions. Teams with an interpersonal advisor and facilitator quickly experience the benefits of cooperation.

The advent of teams leads to a greater openness in all areas of the business. Approaches such as open-book management and the learning company approach discussed in Chapter 3 are often seen when the level of cooperation within an organization increases.

Creativity rises when cooperation increases—a company sees the number and magnitude of new ideas increase. Not only are there more new ideas, but they move forward for management consideration and, eventually, faster and easier implementation than in the past.

A manager sensitive to higher levels of cooperation in an organization encourages organizational approaches to support greater creativity. He or she might bring in creative facilitators or professional idea generators to show the way to generating new ideas. Once the methods are learned, internal resources can lead the way.

To further the development of cooperation, an organization considers loosening the formal policy restrictions. It might be something as simple as allowing more casual dress, or more formal, such as increasing managers' financial spending flexibility.

Discovering the Power of Cooperation—Inspired by a True Story

A few months after Jean had started working at the beverage company, she realized it had very strictly maintained divisions between functions. Every time she tried to get assistance from different functions, she always encountered great reservations.

Jean had a new product idea that she knew would be developed very slowly, if at all in the current system. She knew that she needed to have cooperation among the various divisions in order for the product to have any chance of success.

To work around the company's existing systems, she had to build relationships. She began by inviting her peers who worked in different functions to lunch one at a time. While the primary purpose was to get to know each other better, she knew that she wanted to build trust quickly so that they would be willing to cooperate with her later. During the course of these lunches, she learned a lot about the people and the company. She learned that many of her peers were frustrated by a culture that discouraged cooperation.

After several months of building relationships, Jean decided it was time to act. She invited Joe from package design and Susan from product development to a meeting. She then took the bold step of inviting John from their advertising agency to join them. She outlined her idea for a new product at this meeting. She had done copious consumer research, which suggested the idea had promise. Her initial concept for the product sparked considerable interest among those at the meeting.

After briefing everyone, Jean laid out her plan. She suggested they develop a prototype product, package, and advertising concept as a group. Everyone in the meeting realized this was unprecedented. The accepted practice was that they would each work individually without any knowledge of what the other functions were doing. Their initial reluctance was quickly overcome by their enthusiasm for the idea.

After a few minutes of discussion about their reservations, there was a moment of silence as people considered what they wanted to do. Jean was pleased that everyone signed on.

The discussion quickly moved to next steps. Everyone contributed and listened to the other person's situation. They agreed to have weekly meetings where each team member would share their progress. As a result, Susan from product development would be involved in reviewing package design concepts for the first time in her career. Representatives from the advertising agency were excited because they had an opportunity to influence the final product and package design.

Joe was so excited that at their next meeting he brought seven package design concepts to share with the group. There was spirited discussion about each of them. Before they were done, the group indicated its support for five of them and suggested another three that Joe might pursue. Susan brought the first product prototypes and everyone had a chance to taste the new beverage. Not everyone liked the products, but Susan received some valuable feedback from the group.

At the end of this first meeting, Jean asked everyone how they felt about the process. In her few months at the company, Jean had never seen such big smiles. Everyone felt exhilarated by the interaction. People who had been cooped up in their functional responsibilities felt the power of cooperation for the first time, and they liked it.

The collaboration led to the development of a low-cost prototype television commercial. While the ad was not used, everyone got a big smile from seeing themselves in the ad. It helped emphasize how committed everyone was to making the project a success.

It took several months to develop the project far enough for the entire team to present it to the senior management. For the first time senior management saw the fruits of cooperation. Senior management saw a well-developed new product idea that had been brought to life by advanced versions of product, packaging, and marketing.

This trailblazing effort did not go unnoticed. A couple of years later, this type of cooperation was often required for most projects.

While this type of cooperation is not new to many companies, a large number of companies were founded and have prospered in a very closed, uncooperative environment. For companies that have experienced the power of cooperation, the closed, uncooperative environment seems like the Dark Ages.

Marsha Everton, Vice President of Pfaltzgraff, a Leading Fine China Company

Pfaltzgraff is a family owned and managed company that takes great pride in its fine china and related products—and in its people. It is constantly adding new chapters to that tradition.

This high-quality company attracted Marsha Everton to help the current generation make its mark. Before we get too deep into that part of the story, it helps to understand her roots.

Marsha Everton grew up at ground zero of some of the most uncooperative events of the tumultuous 1960s and 1970s. She lived in Montgomery, Alabama, during the Rosa Parks–inspired demonstrations of the late 1960s and early 1970s. Everton recalls seeing lines of police, some with dogs straining hard on their leashes.

In the 1970s, she lived in the Panama Canal Zone when Panamanians demonstrated for the return of the canal to local control. She remembers being confined to the American sector and having school canceled because of the dangers. Her family filled their bathtub with water fearing the poisoning of the American water supply.

She lived in Washington, D.C., during the Vietnam protests. She recalls the masses of people in and around the city, including many homeless people. This was tough for her, since her father served tours of duty in Vietnam as an Air Force pilot.

Living through only one of these events as a child would make a strong impression and mold the future. Marsha recognizes this: "This string of events was important in my life in ways I might not fully appreciate or know," she says. "It was very powerful to see how committed people could be to a cause."

As powerful as it was, she recognizes the contribution it made to her future life, "One of the great, great gifts from my parents is that I was subjected to so much change," she says. "That has made me so adaptable as an adult. It gave life such texture."

Later in life she developed a deeper sense of how these events helped her, "I really figured out that working with people was important. Maybe that came from the riots I lived through."

Besides these events, some teachers helped mold what she became. She especially remembers her high school calculus teacher, Mr. Brown, who she recalls helped her learn and to do her best. She had to get up in front of the class and teach on occasion.

While her father was away more than most with military duties, he taught her some valuable lessons. One of the more memorable was when he taught her to perform a tune-up on her souped up 351 Mustang. "My father never treated me as a boy or a girl," she recalls. "I didn't get the sense that you had to be this way or that way. I was as likely to be taught how to bake brownies as I was how to tune the car." She had her own timing light and tools. The benefit of this was clear, "I developed the self-confidence that you can take care of yourself."

She entered Georgia Tech as 1 of 60 women—the first women ever admitted to the school. She graduated *magna cum laude* in applied biology in two and a half years, despite working a variety of part- and full-time jobs to fund her education. Her short undergraduate career included coursework at the University of Valencia in Spain.

She applied directly to several graduate business schools and was accepted by Stanford's MBA program, when they were still accepting people directly from undergraduate school. She wanted to go to Stanford because the school was strong in organizational development and interpersonal dynamics. She received a one-year delay in her admission so that she could earn money to help pay for her education at one of America's best and most expensive schools. While at Stanford she focused on strategy, marketing, and finance. She joined and was a cochairperson of the Committee on Corporate Responsibility.

After graduation, she joined Corning Glass in Corning, New York. Befitting her education, she worked in a variety of positions in the company, including product manager, and in finance, technical, and plant positions.

In 1983, after seven years at Corning, she joined Pfaltzgraff. Founded in the early 19th century by German potters, the company has positioned itself as a company with "Old World craftsmanship and unyielding commitment to quality." Today it is the oldest continually operating pottery company in the United States and one of the two leading American manufacturers of ceramic dinnerware and accessories. The company is family owned, now in the fifth generation of management.

In the mid-1990s senior management tapped her to lead a company-wide reengineering project. It was a big project, certainly the biggest company-wide effort in the last decade. It was a full-time assignment for Marsha and eight peers from other departments, plus six part-time members. They also had the assistance of two consulting groups. Their mission was to reinvent the company so that it could effectively compete in a changing and growing environment.

The group's first meeting was filled with anxiety and some discord. Her peers from other departments around the company knew what reengineering could mean—fewer jobs, reassignments, sometimes to lower positions, and an extended period of uncertainty. Her peers were the top talent from all the major departments in the company. The company asked her to be the leader among peers.

On Marsha's life path, she had seen far greater periods of anxiety and differences resolved peacefully. She knew the project's success depended on forging cooperation between people who begin with disparate, competing, and sometimes antagonistic views.

From the beginning, she embarked on a series of team-building exercises. It was not easy going, especially during the first series of meetings. A fellow team member later commented on the kinds of skills that enabled her to ultimately create a very cooperative team, "She is very inclusive. She constantly seeks the opinions of others. She always reaches out to others and uses this skill to reach out over various functions to solve a problem. She is also very humble and down to earth, even though she has a senior title and strong position in the company."

There were days when things did not go well. Yet throughout the process, Marsha remained steady and upbeat. This quality seems to pervade her life. A friend of 18 years observes, "She is unflappable. She does not panic. She doesn't disappear when times are tough."

Another clue to Marsha's success at getting people to cooperate comes from a broader life view she possesses. A close friend describes it, "She has a life philosophy that everything will work out. Marsha believes that you roll with the punches because things will work out. That philosophy consoles her and makes her less afraid in life."

Six months after they started, the reengineering group gained management agreement to a far-reaching plan. There was a fundamental realignment of the company's strategy to be much more consumer-driven. The result was one operating division instead of three. They also focused on the channels through which consumers could buy their products.

The changes had been precipitated by rapid growth in recent years and small, incremental changes over the years that had not been coordinated resulting in patchwork changes. As a result, the processes were not functioning smoothly and required sweeping changes. Some staff reductions came from consolidating three divisions into one and the elimination of duplicated functions. With agreement to the group's proposals, Marsha became vice president of corporate development, where she was responsible for implementing the changes.

Now Marsha is vice president in charge of Pfaltzgraff's retail stores and direct marketing programs. She has worked there since 1983. She was first made a vice president in 1987 and has since held positions in market planning and administration, bone china, consumer products, group vice president of marketing, and corporate development, before her current assignment.

Just as Marsha has flourished at Pfaltzgraff, so has she benefitted her community. She is deeply involved in the community—founding member of Women's Leadership Forum, the Girl Scout Council, and of a variety of church and other activities.

Marsha's career and who she is as a person is a work in progress. She possesses wonderful qualities that make her an exceptional and special person.

Kit Lane, who met Marsha when she was a client, experienced her special qualities first-hand. Three years after she met Marsha, Lane and her husband found themselves caring for three grandparents in their home. All were ill, some gravely, and required round the clock care. The experience was often overwhelming and emotionally draining. Marsha came into this situation and offered some very special help. Here is how Kit describes Marsha's help:

> She made what were tremendously helpful, I mean in the most concrete ways, suggestions of paths for us to take. She did research for us on support systems. We were emotionally caught up. She was tremendous in helping us think straight and she never wasn't really there. It was an exhausting time. She was my rock. I could either vent with her over the sadness of the things that were happening to people I loved or I could turn to her when we needed financial support paying the bills for the care. She would figure out who we should talk to and where we should go. It was the most solid kind of friendship support. Of all our friends, Marsha was the one who could think the most practically when we really could not do it for ourselves. It was a wonderful gift. She made such a tremendous contribution to our lives. This happened only about three years after we met.

Marsha describes her key strength as the ability to think outside the box. Kit has consistently experienced this skill, "When I have a problem, she will tell me another way to think about it. Invariably, we end up laughing like hell at the problem that I thought was unsolvable or unbearable. She is going to help me live with it." Clearly, this ability to be an innovative thinker has enabled her to achieve success at Pfaltzgraff. While holding numerous key positions in her tenure, she has seen sales grow 257 percent.

Recently, Marsha determined there was a major opportunity to gain new consumer understandings. Realizing the company would not fund the very innovative ideas she had, she went to the industry association, an organization where she had, and has, a leadership role. She convinced them to do some very innovative consumer research that involved using anthropologists. They went into people's homes to conduct the research and developed some valuable new insights into consumer behavior. Based on my quarter century of marketing and consumer research experience, this was a very innovative and powerful approach to a challenging consumer problem.

This research led to an industrywide initiative to establish the first National Family Day on March 26, 2000. Marsha was a key person in championing this idea. Her company's focus is on meal time, a key time to bring the family together.

Marsha combines her innovative thinking with extraordinary interpersonal skills. We saw some of them in the reengineering project, but there is more. She describes herself as positive and constructive in her relationships, and clearly others experience this. Coworker Julie Lichty describes Marsha during the toughest times on the reengineering project: "No matter how bad it got, Marsha kept smiling and offering encouragement that we were going to get through it. She never lost the enthusiasm and positive attitude. She was the top role model."

Julie also experienced another one of Marsha's special qualities, "She cares enough to mentor other people. She gives a lot as a mentor. She is not threatened at all by others. She will tell you how good you are and then help you to get even better." She adds, "She really recognizes and compliments people— verbally and in writing. She really lets people know how much she appreciates them." Kit Lane has experienced this away from business, "She does not do people in for her own gain. I learned from how she treated situations that she really cares about other people. She is a responsible person."

Qualities like this resulted in her receiving the Pennsylvania's Best 50 Women in Business Award.

Marsha is a remarkable person—at every stage of life she has been very successful. Her ability to generate cooperation among diverse and competing groups when her company most needed it is only part of the story. She connects with people in a way that trust quickly emerges. She can be of immense help to people when they most need it, as we saw in Kit Lane's experience. Most of us would highly value this type of person as a friend or associate.

Concluding Thoughts

From a rational, scientific perspective, it is amazing how overwhelming the evidence is that cooperation produces better results than competition does. For many people who hold competition as a truth and virtue, this is difficult to see and accept. They point to how capitalism, which is rooted in competition, is the winning and dominant economic structure.

All that says to me is that it has done better than some other options. Cooperation, as outlined in this chapter, is not usually attempted.

Think about the qualities already discussed: Competition breeds distrust. Competitors never trust each other. Competition shuts down true listening. To the extent competitors listen, they listen to learn only those things that can harm the opponent. Competition prevents sharing. Competitors do not want to give anything of value to a competitor because they fear, rightfully, that it will be used against them.

As we will learn in later chapters, competition also creates conditions that directly limit humans achieving their full potential by using their higher abilities. Competition creates fear, our single most crippling force. When we experience fear, we revert to our lower, baser abilities. Fear disconnects us from our inner wisdom. Competition also creates a sense of separateness. We come to believe we are different from our competitors, and we usually label that difference as "better."

Both perceptions go against our inner wisdom. Sages, mystics, and spiritual teachers have told us for thousands of years about the unity of all that is. Now science is telling us the same thing. So much more power, joy, and love comes from all of us living as one than comes from living as separate entities who try to be better than each other.

Marsha's example is both remarkable and commonplace. It is not remarkable because many business leaders have faced similar, and even greater challenges, and have done as well or better. What is remarkable is how Marsha came to know the value of cooperation and the skills that she brings to make cooperation possible. Her positive, innovative, and unflappable qualities are so strong as to make them an inspiration for all of us. Marsha, more than most people in this book, is a work in progress. I will continue to watch her steps along the path of life with great interest.

5

SMILES

Wrinkles should merely indicate where smiles have been.

. . . . .

—Mark Twain (Samuel Clemens)

Y es, *smile!* Clearly a part of the wise approach to success is having fun, having a sense of humor, and being able to smile— a lot. If there is trust, sharing, and cooperation, there can be lots of smiling. It feels good and produces wonderful results.

Fortunately, we have many opportunities to smile. We will focus on two of the more important ways we can smile our way to enlightened success—humor and fun.

Smiles and Humor—
The Wisdom Dimension

The noted editor and writer E. B. White observed the spiritual nature of humor in a 1952 *New Yorker* article: "Every American, to the last man, lays claim to a 'sense' of humor and guards it as his most significant spiritual trait . . ."

Some people may not immediately connect smiles and laughter with wisdom teachers, whom we consider to be solemn and serious. Yet, these great teachers deeply understand the wisdom of smiles and humor.

When you have the opportunity to spend time with a wise teacher, you quickly learn the joy they have for life that manifests as smiles, a keen sense of humor, and laughter. If you watch an interview of the Dalai Lama, you notice he loves to laugh and does so easily and quickly.

Another Tibetan is my teacher Sogyal Rinpoche, who is considered a master, or very wise being. His joy and ability to enjoy a good laugh are among some of my strongest memories of him. Once, he explained how we might purchase some printed materials and audiotapes of his teachings with cash or a check. Then he paused, got a big smile on his face and said, "Of course, you can also pay with *Master*Card." He laughed heartily and his students glowed from his expression of joy from having discovered a little humor to share with us.

Anytime I want to bring the energy of joy into my consciousness, I connect with that time. For me, it is very powerful. Sogyal Rinpoche's expression of humor comes from a different place than it does for most of us. His comes from a deep joy of life and connection with the blissful energy. He glows with positive energy. Having studied with him four times in small groups, I learned entirely new dimensions of being human. His compassion, wisdom, and joy inspire me every day of my life; inspire me to realize the great potential I now know to exist in all of us.

Western wisdom teachers also have a good sense of humor. Wayne Dyer, M.D. (author of *Manifest Your Destiny* and *Wisdom of the Ages,* among others), sprinkles humor throughout his talks. He loves to make fun of himself as a parent. He relates the story of getting upset with one of his daughters over the kinds of things most parents get upset about. His daughter's retort that seems quickly cooled his fuming was, "Oh, if only your readers could see the great guru now!"

The Ageless Wisdom also provides some wonderful perspective on the importance of humor. First, "There are two things which every disciple must someday learn . . . One is to cultivate the ability to 'sit light in the saddle' (to use an old proverbial injunction) and the other is to develop a sense of humour, a real (not forced) capacity to laugh at oneself and with the world." Second, "Preserve, my brother, a sense of humour and a tendency to play, bearing in mind that relaxation is . . . a part of the spiritual life . . ."

The Ageless Wisdom also identifies humor as one of the more important qualities as we walk the path of wisdom, ". . . the major prerequisites for successful esoteric work are patience, persistent effort, vision, and sound discriminative judgment. Given these, plus a sense of humor, an open mind and no fanaticism, the disciple will have rapid progress . . ."

Laugh—It's Good for You and Your Business

Humor in business can be lots of fun, and can make for many happy customers.

This can be especially important in a competitive business, like the airlines. One of the most visible fun companies is Southwest Airlines. The company was cofounded in 1971 by Herb Kelleher. Its results are spectacular. In 1997, its sales topped $3.8 billion, up almost 400 percent over the last ten years, while its net income increased by 1,490 percent.

Low fares clearly have been a key to their success, and they are often the cheapest on the routes they fly. But they have numerous other advantages. They handle luggage quickly and they turn around planes fast—often in half the time of other airlines. All this adds up to getting very high marks for on-time performance; accuracy and speed in baggage handling; and overall customer satisfaction. In industry surveys, Southwest typically is number one or very close to the top of the ratings.

While these numbers are good, it may be the personal element that distinguishes Southwest the most. Many companies known for selling at the cheapest prices hire people at low wages who are not the friendliest or most helpful. But at Southwest, the quality of their people is a truly distinguishing characteristic. This is probably most evident immediately after you get on a Southwest flight.

On most airlines, I tune out the safety briefing, but on Southwest I look forward to it. Usually there is some humor, which has most people in the cabin laughing. People listen to the safety briefing who might otherwise tune it out. For many people, this approach converts uneasiness about flying into confidence. It positively differentiates Southwest from other airlines, which are virtually humorless.

This does not happen by accident. When hiring, Herb Kelleher looks for people with a sense of humor. He knows that the required skills all can be trained, but a person's inherent attitude towards life is not easily changed. Humor and a lightness about life builds a sense of community within the company. This helps offset the stress that comes from hard work and staying on or ahead of schedule.

Sprint is another company that had a very positive experience with humor when they opened a new business center in Louisville. People were asked to create "commercials" for internal use and perform skits as a way of conducting training. Like other companies, Sprint knows that humor increases the effectiveness of their training and helps create a more effective customer service representative.

Companies often make effective use of humor at trade shows, where the objective is to attract key customers and to differentiate themselves from the mass of suppliers. GTE used Chicago's Second City comedy improvisation group to achieve a 700 percent increase in quality sales leads. Importantly, the humor integrated GTE's product story throughout the seven-minute routine. Another company used a comedian and magician at its trade show to triple the number of responses versus the previous year, when they took a very straightforward approach.

Humor is terrifically beneficial at conventions. Art James, the former host of TV's *Concentration,* brings a business-adapted version to conventions. He mixes in a company's themes and messages with humor and playing a game with prizes. John Cleese of "Monty Python" fame, provides a comedy service for conventions and businesses. Convention and seminar speakers who add humor to their speeches have fewer people asleep in the audience.

There are also humor consultants who help business bring more humor into everyday and special occasions. Companies like AT&T, IBM, and Price Waterhouse have used humor consultant Bob Basso. A *Wall Street Journal* article reported that humor consultant Judy Carter helps companies deal with higher levels of stress. Specifically, "They are now using comedy to help employees deal with downsizing and other wrenching changes in the workplace . . ."

The examples of humor in business are many, albeit not enough, but the benefits of humor may surprise you:

- Humor is a powerful immune system booster and reduces the hormones (epinephrine and dopamine) that are associated with stress. Humor and laughter lower blood pressure, are an antidote to depression, defuse hostility, and relieve tension. Since laughter increases the oxygen in the blood, it also reduces pain. As a 17th-century physician noted, "The arrival of a good clown into a village does more for its health than 20 asses laden with drugs."

- William Fry, a humor guru and former Stanford psychiatrist, notes that laughing 100 times a day is good exercise—equal to ten minutes of strenuous rowing.
- Humor consultant Fran Soloman notes that humor speeds learning and retention: "When you laugh . . . there is a mind-body association that helps you retain information. . . . The things we remember from the distant past often are those when we were laughing hysterically."
- According to the *Psychotherapy Letter,* humor's psychological benefits include enabling you to "look at a problem from a different point of view, make it seem less serious, and realize opportunities for increased objectivity." Humor ". . . can help release pent-up feelings of anger and frustration in a socially acceptable way, and is often followed by a state of relaxation, and a feeling of reduced tension." Psychological studies have also found humor reduces depression and anxiety and creates a more positive mood.

Your Role—Creating More Smiles at Work

Bringing more humor into business life requires a plan, according to humor consultants. First, you need to look for opportunities to be humorous. It helps if you take yourself lightly, even if you are involved in serious work.

It helps if you develop a humor group. The group can meet at a set time every day to share a joke of the day, which then is disseminated by group members. Taking candid photographs or videos of willing subjects can also be a source of humor. The opportunities are limited only by your imagination.

Humor is universal, but it is also very personal. What one person finds funny another may not, even within the same culture.

As positive as humor can be, its negative aspects can be equally powerful. When people laugh with each other, it brings an organization together. When people laugh at another person or group, humor can be divisive and destructive. A joke that puts down another person or group is not win-win humor, even if the subject of the humor is not present. Humor that criticizes or is negative in any way about another person or group is potentially dangerous. A positive response by others to this kind of humor only encourages other forms of negative behavior toward the person or group. Similarly, teasing can be painful to the person being teased, regardless of how funny we might find it.

Here are some ways to have fun at work:

- To reduce tension, consider hiring a masseuse to do back and shoulder massages. Don't pressure people into participating though. It should be a treat, not an uncomfortable obligation.
- A basketball hoop in the parking lot can make lunch and after-work activities more fun.
- Consider having theme days at work. Beyond casual Fridays, consider all-you-can-eat lunches, Friday donut breakfasts, and Halloween costume contests. The culture of your organization will dictate which ones are right for you.
- Consider putting fun into your mail system. One company delivered memos via Frisbees on Frisbee memo day.
- Consider establishing a bulletin board where cartoons and jokes are posted. Put it in a high-traffic area.

- The culture in some companies and divisions makes establishing bets in association with objectives both appropriate and fun. Sales objectives are some of the best opportunities.
- Ben and Jerry's has a committee, the "joy gang," that distributes joy grants that reward people who bring happiness to their work. The grants can be used for a wide range of purchases, including a massage.

I will add two from my business career. The assistant brand manager at Procter & Gamble (P&G) gave our group names—big guy, medium-sized guy, and little guy (it helped that we were all guys). He also initiated placing little fuzzy creatures in the most unexpected places around the office and cubicles. I would open a fact book or a desk drawer and there one would be. One day, the brand group went to a fancy restaurant for dinner with our wives or significant others. When the waiter delivered my meal, he put it in front of me and then lifted the cover from the meal to reveal only colorful fuzzy creatures on my plate. We were one of the most productive groups in the division and achieved some of the best business results in the brand's history.

After P&G purchased a Coke bottler, we faced the challenge of integrating into one unit a small family run company with a corporate giant. I decided to make it fun. We hired a video crew that went into every department and videotaped the group performing one of the rock songs that supported our theme for an upcoming new product meeting. We encouraged them to have fun—to really rock out. When the tape was played at the meeting, the laughter and cheers were nonstop. The smiles lasted for weeks, and we achieved the highest introductory market share of any of Coke's 500+ bottlers.

Here are some additional facts you might use to convince others about the benefits of fun:

- A Cornell University study concluded that people who saw a funny movie were more creative.
- Accountemps surveyed 96 executives who said that people with a sense of humor did a better job than those without a noticeable sense of humor.
- A couple of thousand years ago Plato said, "One can discover more about a person in an hour of play than in a year of conversation."
- Academic surveys of business consistently find that humor is strongly supported by managers. They feel it increases productivity and generally improves individual performance.

The evidence supporting more smiles in the workplace is very strong. The main barrier for some managers comes from a belief that work, a serious undertaking, is not funny. But seriousness and fun are not mutually exclusive. Work is serious in some regards and delightfully funny in other regards.

We only need to connect with our inner wisdom to know that when we smile and have fun we do our best work in less time. Many managers in today's workplace vastly underestimate the power of fun.

A Lost Smile—
Inspired by a True Story

Ralph's first meeting at his new company was a pleasure for everyone involved. Ralph greeted everyone with a big smile as they came into the room. When he started his presentation, he noted that it was a pleasure to have the opportunity to update senior management on how a major brand was performing.

His positive and enthusiastic energy seemed to lift the spirits of everyone in the room. Even though this major brand was struggling in some areas, Ralph's approach was very positive about the future. These were not just empty words. He creatively outlined several options and the next steps that he would go through to choose the option with the greatest promise.

At the conclusion of the meeting, several senior managers noted how refreshing Ralph's presentation had been. Other managers who had been with the company longer seemed a bit downcast in comparison. The senior managers congratulated themselves on having made a good hiring decision.

The managers who worked for Ralph basked in a glow of attention he had received. When Ralph was in a meeting with senior managers, those who worked for him also seemed to receive better-than-usual treatment. The meetings were more fun, even when there was bad news.

Ralph's peers saw that he seemed to receive special treatment from senior management. Ralph periodically was invited into private meetings with senior managers who typically did not consult with managers at Ralph's level. This inspired some of those managers to become more positive and upbeat in their own interpersonal styles.

The managers in other departments who interacted with Ralph were also impressed by his positive, almost fun management style. Meetings with him were always very constructive and each seemed to set a new record for the number of smiles in a meeting.

During Ralph's first couple of years in this medium-sized company, almost every proposal he made to senior management was agreed to. The agreed to proposals were implemented on time, under budget, and always met or exceeded their objectives. These accomplishments were due in large part to the enthusiastic support Ralph received from other functions in the company.

Over time, senior management seemed to adjust to Ralph's style. Instead of treating him in a somewhat different way, they started to treat Ralph as they did every other employee. No longer was it good enough to implement proposals on time, under budget, and at or ahead of agreed-to objectives. On every project, no matter how well it had gone, senior management never provided any positive comments. They always wondered why Ralph had not done better. In the beginning, Ralph would readily agree that there were opportunities to do better. When he acknowledged this opportunity, he was criticized for not having taken the necessary actions to do better.

Even when the businesses that Ralph was responsible for achieved record market share and profits, senior management never had anything positive to say. For a while, Ralph attempted to be positive and upbeat, as he had been in the past. Sometimes it seemed the more he attempted to be positive, the more senior management wanted to teach him a lesson. That lesson was deeply ingrained in the culture of this company. The lesson was that, no matter how good you did, it was never good enough. Celebrating apparently positive results could only lead to complacency or so senior management thought.

Ralph tried to respond to the new environment, while still attempting to be positive. When one of the brands achieved record market share, just over 50 percent share of their market, Ralph opened his next meeting with a little celebration. He passed out half of a cupcake with a candle in it to each person in the meeting. He indicated that they could only have half of a cupcake now since they only had half of the market. He indicated that he was eager to celebrate with a whole cupcake when they achieved market dominance. Ralph told them this to balance the celebration, hoping it would be well received by senior management. It was not.

Six years later, Ralph looked back at what happened. His first two years had been positive, fun, and highly productive. Over the next six years, everything seemed to slip from positive to neutral sometimes, but mostly negative. Clearly, the honeymoon had ended a long time ago.

Managers who had been there ten years or more congratulated him on a two-year honeymoon. They told Ralph that in most cases it lasted six months or less.

Over the last six years, Ralph clearly saw that his creativity and effectiveness had dropped. Meetings with senior management that had been fun were now struggles. Ralph had looked forward to these meetings but now dreaded them. The smiles and fun had been replaced by struggle and defensiveness. Ralph deeply resented the transformation because it ran counter to everything he thought life should be.

Not surprisingly, Ralph slowly started to disconnect from his work. It took a couple of years, but others clearly noticed the change. It wasn't long before Ralph started to consider leaving the company. Deep down, he realized that he thrived in an environment where he could be positive, have fun, and do his best. Shortly after this realization, Ralph left the company.

Richard Tuck, Founder and President of Lander International, a Leading Personnel Placement Company

If you knew that the founder and president of one of America's fastest growing companies (according to *Inc.*) had recently adopted a circus, you would not be surprised to discover that when America Online asked him to describe his job he said, "happiness facilitator."

Richard Tuck is the founder and president of Lander International, the world's largest full-service information services audit resource center. But more on Lander later.

While attending a performance of the Chimera Circus in the summer of 1998, Richard was amazed that there were fewer than 100 people at the show he attended. This circus was a special one, and he is in a position to know, as a circus fan. This circus does traditional acts, like juggling and feats of daring, in a nontraditional way. The acts are woven into a theatrical style show in which all the acts perform. Richard was so impressed by the circus that he came back for several more shows, and each time he brought 10 to 15 people with him.

Eventually he talked with the circus owner, Jim Judkins, and learned that the circus had fallen on hard times. Attendance was low, a promoter they had already paid failed to perform agreed-to services, and future bookings were thin.

Richard came to the rescue, advancing the circus money to help them through their rough times. He then started to look for booking opportunities. One opportunity developed in El Cerrito, the headquarters for Richard's company. The city had traditionally been labeled as a noncircus city because there was no fair grounds to locate a circus. Richard identified a mall parking lot as a potential location. The mall was very interested and the circus had a great run there and was rebooked for the next year.

He also got to know many of the 100 people in the circus crew. He learned some Spanish and used it to learn that some of the crew had business degrees from their home countries. One of them became instrumental in selling a school district on sponsoring the circus for the first time. Another person had financial training in his home country. Richard helped train him to contribute to the circus.

Jim Judkins later observed, "Richard's number-one skill is the ability to mine for gold. He can see gold where others do not, and he can see the gold in everyone and then help the person see their own potential."

Richard also introduced a new element into the circus routine. When he first suggested that the circus add a private show, for performers and staff only, Jim was very skeptical. Richard's idea was to run a crazy show on Saturday nights where the performers could try out new acts or parody other acts in the circus before other performers. To Jim's surprise, the performers loved the extra show—it didn't hurt that Richard brought in pizzas. Out of this effort, a couple of new acts have already been added to the circus and morale has improved.

During the winter when the circus is not touring, about ten people remain with the circus. Richard uses some extra space in his business to house the crew. Several of them work part-time in the business on special projects to earn extra money.

The circus is certainly great entertainment, but Richard sees a business opportunity. He is planning to conduct training under the big top when the circus is in large cities. He will use his business contacts to attract people to the training, which will involve the circus performers. People attending the training will actually become part of the circus acts for the day to learn certain business principles.

Richard's business success to date has come from founding Lander International, the leader in placing electronic data processing (EDP) auditors in businesses. An article in *Inc.* shared the comment of another recruiter in the field, "From the standpoint of a recruiter, if Richard is working for a client, you are probably not going to bother to compete against him, because you are going to lose."

After he stopped teaching English in high school, Richard took a job in personnel services. He saw that the company's focus was on having people make a certain number of calls per day and achieving set quotas. So he convinced the company to *not* train him. Instead, he focused on the clients and their needs, in effect bonding with clients. His approach was so effective that eventually the company changed its hiring and training practices.

Despite the progress and success, it was not enough for Richard, so he started his own company, first called Paramount Personnel Services. He started it with a vision and two days' planning. He was immediately successful and recalls that success came in part because he did not know better. When he wanted to add an executive recruiter to the staff, she insisted on changing the company name to something she would be more comfortable with. Lander was chosen because it was her maiden name; International, because they were making international placements. Given Richard's sense of fun, when he is asked where the name came from he is tempted to buy a portrait of a stuffy old gentleman, place it in the lobby, and invent a story about Alfred Lord Lander—but he has not succumbed yet.

While the business was successful from the start, over a period of several years, he found himself becoming less happy. The hours became longer and he found himself hiring people with prior sales experience, something every company in the business did. But Richard found that these people were more focused on their personal successes and less on truly understanding the customer.

Eventually, Richard decided he was not having fun and that there must be a better way. Not knowing exactly what that was, he left to tour Europe, leaving the company in the hands of a hired manager. When he returned, he began working from his home instead of working in the office. When he quickly found himself earning more money than all the other people in the office combined, he decided a major change was needed. He moved the offices closer to his home, which caused all but two people to leave, and began working alone for several years. He had success and fun again.

When Richard saw the opportunity to grow by adding people to the business, he adopted an entirely different recruiting and hiring approach. He ran teaser ads that did little to define the job but created a sense of excitement and fun. When people interviewed, he explored what they wanted to do in life; if he wanted to hire them, he looked for ways to adapt his opportunity to their needs. The result was that he hired people he liked, people who were genuinely nice and that he enjoyed working with. Another major change was that he did not hire people with previous sales experience, instead hiring people with diverse backgrounds. One staffperson is a former concert bass trombonist; another person makes furniture out of driftwood and works at Lander to fund his craft.

This approach has resulted in several million dollars of sales and a 994 percent revenue jump between 1993 and 1997. Today Richard is certainly having fun. To get each day off to the right start, he will play games, Nintendo and others, for example, before he goes to work.

If you were only familiar with Richard's years as a kid, you might guess that he would not be successful at much of anything. He notes his family was dysfunctional on many levels. His mother was married eight times, his father six. Later in life he determined that every six months of his early years, he got a new parent on one side or moved or changed schools or had a new housekeeper, who was often the dominant person in the house. In addition, no one in the household had graduated from high school. It is no surprise that Richard concludes, "I grew myself up" during all these years.

At a very early age, he took charge of his life in a fun way. In his words, "I discovered that I really enjoyed entertaining others, helping them find happiness. Maybe because I wasn't terribly happy, I sort of escaped and found out that it was really fun to make others happy and that made me happy."

Richard acted on this insight in a fun way. He started by putting on magic shows for kids in the neighborhood. Then he really started to enjoy movies and combined both interests. He bought a very simple projector and started showing silent movies and putting on a magic show at his house on Saturdays, charging a nickel per person. After two Saturdays, he had enough money to buy another film and the shows went on. Today, he has 18,000 films in his collection. At one time, he even taught college courses on motion picture appreciation.

Since his childhood environment was not the most positive one, he did some escaping, but in very constructive ways. One way was by developing a love of writing. By fifth grade, he had written 13 novels. He would also escape by diving into his class work, "When I came home from school, my household really was not good, so I would escape from it. So I would just go into my own little world. If the teacher gave a homework assignment, I would do 10 homework assignments. If the task was to look a word up in the dictionary and write out its definition, I would write out 100 words."

This focus on school had an impressive result—Richard graduated from high school when he was 15 and immediately began college. After graduating from college, he went to get his master's and teaching credential in one year, which required completing 64 units. He knew at an early age that he wanted to pursue teaching because teachers were the only adults he admired. He modeled his life on teachers because a teacher would never smoke, swear, drink or any of those kinds of things. He observed, "I equated these with being a good adult." While he went on to teach in high school for only three years, he still considers one of his key business roles to be as a teacher.

Richard also believes a responsible adult helps others. He usually helps people at his house, which is affectionately known as "it's gotta be magic." He has turned much of the house into a fun place to be—there are rooms dedicated to Disney, Broadway plays and Hollywood, pinball machines, a theater viewing room, and a magic stage. The house has become a tourist attraction, with 3,000 visitors a year.

Into this wonderful environment he invites many groups of needy people. They will dedicate a whole day to the homeless or cancer victims or people with AIDS. When at the house, guests are treated like kings and queens, fed from a wonderful banquet and entertained by Richard, who is a natural entertainer. Visitors have been known to laugh more than they ever have and to leave with tears of joy, saying that was to best day of their lives.

When my daughter left his house, she was as excited and full of positive energy as I have ever seen. Richard's house is a truly remarkable experience. We have tried several times to describe it to others, but the descriptions always fail to capture the magical qualities he has designed into his house.

Richard understands himself well and is constantly working to understand himself better and use that to create more happiness. In 1998, he consulted a Jungian astrologer in whose insights surprised him, but also resonated with truth.

The insights had two main themes. Richard describes the first one: "I am a strongly empathic person. I can feel people's pain. I tend to be a real detective. I tend to want to find out who the real person is inside." His empathy manifests itself in his hiring policies where he wants to adapt a job to a person, his business practices where he takes a humanistic approach with people in the recruiting process, and with his help for those less fortunate than him.

The second insight is that he is a heroic leader. He is a hero in ways we do not always recognize as heroic. He has the courage of his convictions and acts on them even when they are at odds with how other people think things should be done.

Even people outside the business world recognize Richard's natural leadership skills. Richard has served as a juror nine times. Each time dressed very casually, like he does every day, in jeans and a T-shirt. Each time he barely communicated with other jurors as he listened intently and took notes during the trial. And each time, he was quickly elected jury foreman, a position he never sought. This defies random chance and suggests there is an attractiveness about him that easily enables people to sense he is a leader. Thomas Leonard, founder of Coach University, is a strong proponent of attracting people by being who we really are. When we do this, people recognize those qualities and are drawn to them.

Richard also has the ability to create a dynamic vision. A friend of 25 years observes, "Richard believes if you can imagine something, you can do it. He thinks of a lot of things that other people don't. And even if other people did think them, they would think they could not be done." Richard recognizes his abilities and is confident in them. "Throughout all of my life," he says, "I have always trusted my abilities, zeal, and enthusiasm."

Richard's home has a wonderful view of a prominent mountain in the area that looms over the Bay Area's fog. One morning not long ago, looking out over the foggy landscape, he noticed the sky was a dark blue, in stark contrast to the pure white of the fog. It was almost as if he could walk across the fog to the mountain in the distance.

In this setting, he experienced a vision of his future. He observed, "I should be figuring out how to share more joy with people. I have a special gift and I should be doing something with it. I have always been weird and precocious. I should use that. I shouldn't be holding back or stifling who I am with a business career." He has numerous specific ideas, which he is now acting on. Not surprisingly, the circus came into his life for a reason. It is part of a broader vision of how he can be a true happiness facilitator. It will be very interesting to learn how his vision has progressed five years from now.

He concluded with what may be the true theme of his life and great advice for all of us: "Don't waste your life doing things that are not meaningful to you. Get out there and have fun. Explore what you are here for. We're in such a golden age where there is opportunity everywhere."

This is the message I suggest we take from Richard's example. He is in touch with his life vision and he is actively living it. He is a "happiness facilitator." Each of us has our own vision and our challenge is to discover it and live it. When we follow our own guiding light, life is filled with joy and fun, and we experience life as effortless.

Concluding Thoughts

For people who have not experienced the positive power of smiling and fun, this may seem like a frivolous chapter. Those who have had fun and smiles at work know how powerful happiness can be. That power makes every other skill and quality much more effective. It is like a turbo booster on an engine.

During my business career, I experienced periods of smiles and fun. I shared some of those periods earlier. All of those periods are associated with dramatically improved business results. People do their best when they have fun. It is that simple.

But having fun in most businesses, unfortunately, is not a simple endeavor. So many myths associate smiles with a lack of seriousness or caring. People who have not experienced the power of smiles perpetrate these myths. Their beliefs may come from those moments of humor and fun that are at the expense of the company. If so, it is symptomatic of a situation where the other wise success qualities are missing. For example, where trust is low, people may express their displeasure with leaders or the company through biting, sarcastic humor.

When this occurs, it reinforces an important point. For fun and smiles to be a major constructive force, the other qualities contributing to wise success need to be in place. There needs to be trust, listening, sharing, and cooperation.

Richard Tuck may be the most remarkable person in this book. He certainly has the most fun. I suggest that his example is not that we should all set goals of riding every roller coaster in America, adopting a circus, and turning our house into a tourist attraction. Certainly, if these goals excite you, then go for them.

Richard's example inspires me to live my passions; to do what really gives me joy. That can be different in its specifics for most of us. He knows that he wants to make others happy. He does that by helping people have fun. He makes business fun and his away-from-business time also is dedicated to fun. For him, there is little distinction between work and the rest of his life.

6

BALANCE AND WHOLENESS

Assume preference for being a whole person.

• • • • •

—One of Abraham Maslow's keys to enlightened management,
Maslow on Management

Today, more than ever, a balanced life is seen as a key to success. In a few years, having a whole life will supersede balance as the standard for many, if not most people. Creating a balanced life is an interim step on the way to creating a whole life.

Being in balance generally means we dedicate quality time to the various parts or roles in our life. Having a whole life means there is a total integration of our various roles. What we once viewed as parts of a life are now a seamless whole life.

Many factors are driving the desire for balance and a whole life. One is the recognition that there is actually more to life than just work. The promise of happiness coming just from our work is rapidly diminishing, especially among younger Americans.

A Profound Shift—
The Need for Balance

For the first time, survey firms like Roper Starch and Yankolovich conclude more people rate their nonwork time as more important than work time. For decades, people rated work time as much more important than nonwork time.

I experienced this profound shift as a senior corporate manager in the 1980s and 1990s. New hires from the nation's top business schools no longer automatically put in 60-plus-hour weeks. Instead, their nonwork time was a major topic of discussion and focus of their energy.

The most vivid tug-of-war over whether work or nonwork was most important took place over a business lunch. People subscribing to the old view were very uncomfortable talking about anything other than work-related subjects. People with the new view saw lunch as part of their personal time and pushed the discussion to sports, politics, or fun times at every opportunity.

The need and struggle for balance happens at all levels of business. Senior executives, many who are on the fast track to the top, resign to spend more time enjoying the personal and family parts of their life. For example, Aetna president Joseph Sebastianelli resigned from his high-paying, senior position because it conflicted with his family life. The desire to help two teenage sons was a powerful factor in his decision. There are many more stories like this, from large companies like Pepsi and Procter & Gamble to much smaller companies.

From another perspective, the people left behind after a downsizing have to do the work of the people who left, in many cases exacerbating already out-of-balance lives.

People are responding in a number of ways, in many cases starting their own companies. While there are several factors behind the growth in new and home-based companies, one factor is people's desire to create a work life that accommodates and nurtures the other parts of their life.

The move toward a balanced life is seen vividly in studies of business school graduates, the future leaders in business and industry. A 1996 study by Coopers & Lybrand revealed business school graduates ranked "ability to achieve a balanced lifestyle" as one of the three most important considerations in choosing a company at which to work, equal in importance to salary and management opportunities. Other studies confirm the desire by recent graduates to have it all. There is a strong expectation that a full personal life and work success are compatible objectives.

Another aspect of these emerging attitudes is the desire by a growing number of students to work for socially responsible companies. Mark Albion, a former Harvard marketing professor, cofounded Students for Responsible Business (SRB), whose members hail from more than 100 top business schools. In an SRB study, many members revealed a willingness to work for a lower salary if it meant they could work for a socially responsible company. The interest in social responsibility is an aspect of the desire by an increasing number of students to evaluate work in the context of their whole life and its impact on the lives of others. Albion also plans to form a headhunting company to link people with socially responsible companies.

The interest in working for social responsibility is also found among senior managers who leave high-paying positions to work for socially responsible companies. For example, William Haber, one of the three founders of Creative Artists Agency—at its peak, the most powerful company representing Hollywood stars—left this very lucrative business and his Beverly Hills lifestyle to join the Save the Children Federation, headquartered in Connecticut.

Balance—The Personal Perspective

The need and drive to bring balance into our life comes from deep within. Maybe we have lived an out-of-balance life—

making every possible sacrifice for work, for example, thinking it is the path to success and happiness, only to discover it is not. We may have observed parents who sacrificed time with family and other roles in their lives to make money and financially support the family, only to be unhappy and burned out early in life. We decide either that enough is enough or that dedicating so much to work is not for us.

We get to a point where we agree with psychologist Barbara Killinger, Ph.D., as quoted in Stephen Covey's *First Things First:*

> Wisdom comes from . . . balance. Workaholics are very intelligent, interesting, often witty and charming people, but they lack this inner wisdom. The crises in their lives attest to this. Good judgment comes when your rational and logical thoughts are supported by a gut reaction that the decision "feels" right, and you can live comfortably with the consequences of your decision. Inner wisdom goes even farther because the decision not only feels right, but it also fits with your values and beliefs. Something deep inside you can answer "Yes!"

In our heart, we now know what Ghandi knew when he said, "One man cannot do right in one department of life whilst he is occupied with doing wrong in another department. Life is one indivisible whole."

For most of us the "departments" are the physical, mental, spiritual, social, and emotional parts of our life as they play out in our various roles—employee/business owner, parent/spouse/significant other, and community volunteer, for example. For there to be balance, these dimensions need regular quality time.

But we do not set out to achieve balance in our life for the sake of balance itself. Rather, it is what balance brings us that is important. One of the people I respect the most is Susan Smith

Jones, Ph.D., who has written several very practical books on how to achieve balance. She captures the benefit of achieving balance in this observation from *Choose to Live Peacefully:* "Being successful is not a matter of how much money you have, how many possessions you've collected, or what type of lifestyle you live; success can be measured only to the degree to which you have inner peace and, no matter what the circumstances or situation, you can remain peaceful, calm, and happy."

Inner peace is a powerful benefit of life balance. Only when we can will ourselves to feel peace within and when peace is the pervasive undercurrent to all our actions can we truly have inner peace. For many people, inner peace is associated with a consciousness of a higher power in the universe. Before achieving this high level of inner peace, we may experience moments of treasured inner peace, which we gradually may learn to extend into our whole life. With inner peace comes previously elusive happiness we seek.

Inner peace comes from bringing at least two experiences into our life. First, we develop a deep sense of wholeness, connectedness, or sense of unity with all that is. This experience links us to our world as a partner—we're no longer combatants in the Darwinian world where everything can be a potential threat to our survival. Second, we stop feeling needy. To do this, we meet or eliminate our emotional, mental, and physical needs. No longer do nagging drives result in bad choices. Associated with this we also eliminate the tolerations (things we put up with that don't help us) in our life, a powerful relief and calming force for many people.

While achieving inner peace can certainly be classified as an honorable life goal, it brings with it significant additional benefits. Inner peace helps us make better decisions in all areas. The inner peace enables us to perceive more—we are not distracted by the inner clamor of mind chatter.

With inner peace, we connect with our inner wisdom, our intuitive ability, and can hear its quiet voice. Intuition, we will discover, is the higher-mind ability where synthesis takes place. When we make decisions guided by our higher mind, we select win-win solutions, the best solutions to whatever problem we face. When we bring this ability to business issues, we make better decisions with much less effort. It will take some time, but eventually even business managers will recognize that they don't do their best work when stoked on adrenaline and under high stress.

Two powerful trends today support the quest of inner peace as a way to achieve life balance. The first is the rapidly emerging efforts of many people to simplify their lives. While this appears to be a new idea, the wisdom of this direction has existed for centuries. Plato wrote more than 2,000 years ago, "In order to seek one's own direction, one must simplify the mechanics of ordinary, everyday life." And over 150 years ago, Henry David Thoreau wrote, "Our life is frittered away by detail. . . . Simplify, simplify."

The current movement to simplify life has spawned books, newsletters, and media articles along with an enthusiastic band of converts. As a member of that group, I found amazing benefits from our two-year simplification effort. We sold two homes. One was a home we had bought for family members who no longer needed it, and a second was a mountain weekend and vacation home that we frequently used. We also sold our primary home and bought a new one that was 50 percent smaller. Whew! Fewer yards, roofs, appliances, etc., screaming for attention. The smaller primary home was perfect for our needs—why hadn't we done it much sooner? Other efforts like scaling down to less expensive cars and eliminating negative relationships transformed our lives. There was now space for those things that were important to me—two hours each day for meditation, for example.

Closely coupled to simplification is structure and guidance to help people create needed balance. *The Seven Habits of Highly Effective People* was a major first step for many people in getting the guidance that made a difference in their life. Covey's advice to be proactive, to think win-win, and to first seek to understand and then be understood has resonated with millions of readers.

Covey's next book was dedicated to one of these seven habits—"first things first." The underlying advice in the book came from a quote from Goethe: "Things which matter most must never be at the mercy of things which matter least." As a companion to the book, he developed the next generation time management system. This system recognized the various roles we play and made spending quality time on all the roles as routine as people had previously done for just their role in business. The system also included the advice to "sharpen the saw," or to have an ongoing personal growth program.

Beyond Balance—A Whole Life

Have you ever heard someone say, "I am a completely different person when I am away from work"? And they are! They have departments and roles in their life that have little in common with each other. We see a person described very differently by a close business associate, a close away-from-work friend, and a parent, for example. Often this consciously occurs because of a feeling that there are risks in letting the roles overlap too much.

A whole life occurs when the barriers come down and there is great interplay and connection between all our roles. We love our job because it enables us to, as the Army ads say, "Be all you can be." We are living a dynamic vision of our purpose in life. We are now clear and confident in who we are. Having achieved the inner peace associated with balance, we connect with our inner essence and live that essence or spirit all the time, in all of life's roles. These powerful changes happen over a decade or longer.

When we live from essence, we no longer change faces as we move from role to role in life. We are the same person with everyone. We are confident and have nothing to hide. We are guided by an inner compass and no longer need the validation of others to feel good about who we are. We see the world as one undifferentiated whole that includes us. When this occurs, we have a whole life. It goes beyond balance, because our life roles are now seamlessly intertwined.

Your Role—Creating More Balance in Business

New employee benefit programs and policies have emerged over the last two decades to help employees—especially two-income families with kids—more effectively cope with life's stresses and complexities. An entire new industry has emerged from this trend—services that help companies provide life-balance support to their employees. Businesses have done all this because it is ultimately good for their financial results.

The following are just some of the life-balance programs companies provide their workers:

- Silicon Graphics offers a paid six-week sabbatical after every four years of company service.
- Hewlett-Packard offers a one-year leave of absence with complete medical coverage and a guaranteed job when you return.
- Cisco provides an early morning boot camp class, a daily one-hour workout program, in company facilities.
- Sun Microsystems offers a special menopause counseling program.
- Cigna, Aramark, and Amgen have experimented with programs where their cafeterias offer employees the opportunity to take home an evening meal.
- Many companies allow people to take vacation days in less than full-day increments—even an hour at a time.

- Flexible time has become a regular program at many companies. The intent is to help employees balance their work and family commitments. Some companies extend the concept to accommodate a shift from full to part-time jobs and telecommuting.
- Childcare is another staple at many companies, with many offering onsite facilities. One of the more innovative is Dutton's Brentwood Books in Los Angeles that has on onsite program that includes young babies.
- A Los Angeles ad agency has a goal of only hiring people who live close to the agency so people will not burn out from the long, agonizing commutes for which LA is infamous. This agency prides itself in not having people working late into the night or on weekends.
- Mattel offers 16 hours a year of paid time off for school-related activities.
- There are unusual benefits—a music store in Southern California that offers to pay for tickets to rock concerts, and an information technology company in Minneapolis that has surprise outings to go parasailing or play laser tag. It is not clear whether these are really balance programs, but they are fun.

Companies have begun to take pride in these benefits. This pride often translates into intense competition for the awards given for the best companies to work for based on various balance and family criteria. Three major magazines annually recognize companies—*Fortune* (Best Companies to Work For), *Business Week* (Best Companies for Work and Family), and *Working Mother* (Best Companies for Working Mothers). The U.S. Department of Labor got into the act with its Honor Role of 770 employers with policies that are friendly to families and women and the Ron Brown Award, recognizing excellence in employee and community relations, that they hope will become as prestigious as the annual Baldrige Award for quality and excellence.

Among the new companies whose primary mission is to provide benefits that help employees balance their lives is Work-Family Directions, Inc., which offers a wide range of services for education and older parents, as well as personal services and services to balance your life through its LifeWorks programs. Most of its innovative programs focus on the employee's stage of life—including help in finding good schools, ways to take a child on a business trip, choosing a therapist, and dealing with senior parent legal and financial issues.

Companies justify the cost of life-balance programs because they reduce costs related to absenteeism, turnover, and stress. Life-balance programs can also make a company more competitive by increasing productivity and attracting more highly qualified employees. As expansive as today's life-balance programs are (compared to 10–15 years ago), they ultimately are guided by what makes financial sense, not by humanitarian instincts or a deep sense of what is right and fair.

The Quest for Balance— Inspired by a True Story

Scott had had it. An accident ahead of him had once again turned traffic into a crawl. His 90-minute work commute was probably going to be closer to two hours today. Usually when Scott was stuck in traffic he would turn up the radio in an attempt to drown out his ever-increasing frustration.

Today was a little different. For the first time he wondered why he was putting up with this. During the last weekend, he had had an interesting conversation with his best friends at their mountain-top home. Scott had always been focused on doing his job rarely thinking about much else. But this past weekend he had started to question the motivation behind his autopilot life.

He reflected on his typical workday. He usually left home at 6:30 AM, his family barely awake, and he dove into the early commuter traffic. After driving a narrow road with many twists and turns, he arrived at the freeway, where he quickly encountered stop-and-go traffic. Since this was Massachusetts, he encountered some of the worst drivers in the nation.

After a long commute, Scott would put in a hard day's work. His rigid type-A personality would leave him worn out by the time he needed to dive into traffic again for the trip home. After another 90-minute drive, he would arrive home at about 7:00 PM, one hour before his young daughter's bedtime. Worn out by the day of work and driving, Scott usually was not very good company after work.

Scott realized he didn't like this picture of his life. While there were incredible levels of business accomplishment, there was not much happiness, let alone joy.

It wasn't until a few years later that Scott realized his mountain-top retreat marked the beginning of a long period of introspection and reflection. Sitting in traffic that morning, Scott realized that his life was much more of a mystery than he had ever imagined. This vague stirring turned into a quest to better understand himself and the world he lived in.

Over the next several weekends, Scott spent time with his family and their best friends. These friends were very much into understanding life and themselves. Long conversations over the dinner table explored a wide range of subjects Scott had never considered before. He learned that his friends had done extensive reading and had attended several inspiring personal growth seminars over the past several years. In addition, they had both worked with a Jungian psychologist in another effort to better understand themselves, which surprised Scott. He had always considered people that see a psychologist as weak. Not only were his friends strong, they also were vibrant, taking on life at full speed.

Scott wondered whether a psychologist could help him. For the next several months, Scott saw their psychologist on a weekly basis. He had an immediate breakthrough in understanding a lifelong repetitive dream that gave him a glimpse into his relationship with his parents.

Scott found this effort to be exhilarating. He loved the conversations and every week he seemed to take a big step forward in understanding things that he had never before considered. Gradually, he started to invest more time in his relationship with his family and his relationships at work became even closer.

Looking back almost 20 years later, Scott realized how important his time being stuck on the freeway had been. Twenty years ago, work took about 90 percent of his waking weekday energy. Now it takes about 50 percent of his time, with his other roles in life taking up the balance of time. The time he spends working now is far more creative and joyful. The other parts of his life have blossomed wonderfully and Scott feels blessed that he had taken the path that he had.

Carol Hess, Director, Workplace Strategies, Kuntz, Lesher, LLP

Carol Hess recently left Lancaster Laboratories, where she was a vice president, to help other companies with the many innovative programs she initiated there.

In 1997, she was *Working Mother* magazine's 1990 Working Mother of the Year and found her life out of balance. She needed more "face time" with her two daughters as they grew older and was stressed by work and her community activities.

Carol approached the president of her company, Lancaster Laboratories, to develop a solution. They quickly agreed to a plan where Carol would leave work at about 3:00 PM three days a week, using a cellular phone and pager to keep her linked to the office in case someone needed her.

It is interesting that the person who put her company on the leading edge of helping employees have balance in their lives found her own life out of balance. But she worked out an innovative solution for her situation, just as she has for her company over almost 15 years. Through her leadership, Lancaster Laboratories opened a day-care center for employees in 1986 that now serves 151 children. Then they built an adult day-care facility for 25 senior citizens, and a 13,000-square-foot fitness center for employees.

Visible initiatives like these have placed the company on *Working Mother*'s top 100 companies for nine consecutive years. It has received several other prestigious awards—*Business Week* designated the company one of the 30 best companies for work and family, *Inc.* magazine designated it one of the best small family-friendly companies, and in 1997 President Clinton awarded the company (Carol accepted for the company) a Special Mention for 1997 Ron Brown Corporate Leadership.

Carol's efforts to help people integrate work, home, and their other roles have been just as innovative in less obvious work-related situations. Shortly after the company went from being a private, family-held concern to a subsidiary of a larger company, a bitter winter significantly reduced sales in what already was the slowest quarter of the year. Not surprisingly, word came down from the parent company to reduce labor costs.

While not a surprise, the company faced an unprecedented challenge; there had never been layoffs when the company was family owned. To have layoffs so soon after the acquisition would have been particularly damaging to morale.

Carol approached this with an open mind and shared the challenge with employees. The result was an innovative solution that saved more than the needed money—without layoffs. The solution was a voluntary time off program where everyone in the company would take three unpaid days off in three months, with no requirement to take the time off.

She recalls that when the program was announced that one employee stood up and said his finances were so tight that he could not afford the three days of lost pay. Another person jumped up and said he would love to take six days off—his three and other person's three. They agreed to do it.

Carol even gave people flexibility about how time off would affect their paychecks. People could take three unpaid days spread over the full three months or take it all in one paycheck. For this situation, she reduced day-care charges for the weeks in which people took their voluntary time off—normally users paid for five days a week whether they used it or not.

At the end of the program, the company had actually saved four days per employee instead of the needed three. Employees so embraced the idea that it became an ongoing benefit program where employees could buy additional vacation time. Today, about 200 employees take advantage of the program annually. So what started out as a potentially unpleasant experience became a very positive one, in large part because of Carol's leadership.

After the experience she observes, "I really believe that all we had to do was tell employees what we needed to do and that everyone would pull together and make it happen." She adds, "I always seem to be able to find a compromise. . . . I have the ability to see things from another person's point of view." This is a great skill that has served her and her company well.

Her parents Earl and Anita Hess founded Lancaster Labs in 1961. Located in Lancaster, Pennsylvania, the company offers analytical and consulting services to the chemical and biological sciences. Its services focus on three areas. First, it does environmental testing, groundwater and hazardous wastes, for example. Second, it tests food products and animal feeds for nutritional content, residues, and so on. It also does testing for many of the nation's leading pharmaceutical companies.

When the company was sold to Thermo Analytical Inc., Carol was the only Hess family member to remain with the new management. She first joined the company in 1981, while still at Ursinus College where she graduated with a BS in applied mathematics and economics. In 1987, she received her MBA from St. Joseph's with a focus in administrative management.

To accomplish what she has, Carol has had to have a strong internal compass, and she feels her values are very clear. She observes, "I have a strong sense of values. There are some things that are not negotiable, especially when it comes to family."

Often values serve us best when they are tested. Consistent with her family-first focus, she says, "I find myself sometimes in a tough situation in business. I need to bend the rules because a person really needs me to bend the rules. Maybe it is going to cost us something today, but in the long term, we are doing the right thing. We need to help this person." She adds, "It is hard for me to follow the rules when someone is going to be hurt by them."

A few years ago when she was interviewing a job candidate, she found her thinking challenged. She found him very qualified for the position and wanted to hire him. But during the conversation, he stated that he was leaving his previous company because he had reached the maximum lifetime insurance limit there because of his daughter's cancer. So he wanted to join a new company with a new maximum limit.

Realizing that hiring this man would result in taking on a very high insurance cost for the company, she did it anyway. Today she concludes, "I don't know what it cost us, but it was worth every penny."

As she looks to the future, she has a clear purpose: "I really do think that my job is to be there to make it easy for people to be successful." There is a clear trend and need that she sees defining future programs, "My ideal is to customize the work environment to each individual employee. It can be in their hours, space, job assignments. They should be doing what they are good at and what they enjoy doing. There is not a fight between home and work. I think this is a lot more feasible than people think."

Concluding Thoughts

Maybe the most profound and underreported shift in American thinking is that we now rate nonwork time as more important than work time. When I entered the workforce in the 1970s, this was almost unthinkable for most, but certainly not all Americans.

Today we want a life that is much more than just work. We want health, so we spend money and time on exercise and its associated equipment, on better foods, and on supplements, especially herbal ones, that promise more and better energy to enjoy life. We want quality relationships, and there are multiple signs those friends and family ties are strengthening for many people. We want calmer, quieter times, and the simplicity and spiritual movements are just two illustrations of where this impetus is taking people.

My sense is that the move to connect with spirit will be the broad and pervasive way most people bring balance into their lives. It leads to a wholeness, a unity that quickly results in going beyond a balanced life with its compartmentalized life roles to the seamless whole life this chapter briefly discusses.

Hess is a leader and a pioneer in helping employees achieve balance in their lives. She has led her company into some of the most innovative ways of helping people do this. What especially impresses me is how her efforts go well beyond what is broadly recognized. To the everyday operations, she brings a constant spirit of wanting to develop win-win solutions to challenging problems. These challenges can involve one person or the entire company. Her purpose is consistent.

Yet, despite her achievements, she found her life to be out of balance. She took innovative and decisive action that had the expected positive results. Like Carol Hess, we have a constant need to monitor how we are doing and how our changing needs affect us. Being in balance or living a whole life is a constant work in progress, even for those who are experts at the process.

7

SPIRIT

- *Assume an active trend to self-actualization.*

- *We must ultimately assume at the highest theoretical levels of enlightened management theory, a preference or a tendency to identify with more and more of the world, or peak experience, cosmic consciousness, etc.*

• • • • •

—Two of Abraham Maslow's keys to enlightened management,
Maslow on Management

A strong spiritual rebirth is taking place. While the rebirth is intensely personal, there are many signs that spirituality and its associated ethics are emerging into public forums, including business. This trend is likely to be a powerful transforming force that ultimately will change the way we conduct business—and our lives. Ralph Waldo Emerson emphasized the importance of the spiritual perspective in life when he said, "Great men are they who see that the spiritual is stronger than any material force."

Of necessity, this chapter touches only on subjects that could be books by themselves. The first part of the chapter discusses the manifestations of the spiritual trend emerging in American culture and society. The second part details some of the major spiritual and ethical tenets put forward by two leading teachers. The last part relates personal stories of spirit in business and life.

Before we embark on this journey, it's important to define *spiritual,* since it is a new and sometimes misunderstood term for some.

A spiritual person is aware of a power in the universe that is greater than himself or herself. We give that power a wide variety of names—God, Spirit, Allah, Tao, Universe, and so on. Others who consider themselves to be spiritual explicitly reject the tenets and constraints of organized religion. As used here, *spiritual* encompasses organized religious activities as well as those that are not codified, ritualized, and labeled—and as a result can be very personal and customized.

Spirituality—It's Everywhere

When TV ads for Campbell's Soup conclude that their product is "Mmm! Mmm! Good for the body, good for the soul," we know that spirituality is entering the mainstream. Of course, this line in part leverages the popularity of the *Chicken Soup for the Soul* books, another indication of spirituality's increasing power.

Other spiritual and quasi-spiritual allusions in advertising include images of people munching Snickers bars at the pearly gates, Volvo's tag line that its car can "save your soul," Volkswagen's ad campaign for its new version of the VW Beetle, first popular in the counterculture 60s and 70s: "If you sold your soul in the 1980s, here's your chance to buy it back," General Foods International Coffees' line, "It stirs the soul," and Allways Natural Aromatherapy Essential Oils' advertising line that it "enriches hair, scalp, skin, and spirit."

Spirituality is also entering other parts of the business world besides advertising. From a very wide view, the naming of Amartya K. Sen as the 1998 Nobel laureate in economics recognizes the importance of morals and spirituality in what is a quantitative science. Sen is known as the Mother Teresa of economics because he brings a moral perspective unique to economics.

Sen argues that well-being should not be measured by wealth alone. He also notes the importance of life expectancy and educational attainment in evaluating economic success. In addition, he makes a powerful point that taking care of a nation's most vulnerable people is actually good for business.

Spirituality is entering individual businesses in a variety of ways. Some companies hire chaplains from companies such as Inner Active Ministries (IAM), founded by Mark Cress, a former CEO of one of America's fastest growing private companies. IAM provides traditional chaplain services to companies in North Carolina's Research Triangle area. His company provides a range of services, including nondenominational bereavement counseling and personal consulting on matters of the spirit. Mark sees $100 million sales potential for his new company.

Religious counseling is also reaching into the boardrooms. Rabbi Visotzky, who conducts regular sessions for CEOs of all denominations, finds the Bible to be an excellent source of business lessons. Specifically, four stories in Genesis and Exodus present rich opportunities for discussion not only of business techniques themselves but of their moral and ethical implications. A recent magazine article noted some CEOs are finding spiritual counseling in a company is more effective than having an ethics officer or statement of ethics that no one reads.

Companies are finding that reengineering and downsizings have left many employees disoriented and demoralized. Many baby boomers are questioning who they are by conducting midlife reviews (that can quickly turn into crises). The goal is to define what they want to do with the rest of their life. Gen X-ers want a holistic workplace that enables them to have a whole life, one in which work is a part and maybe not the most important part.

Craig Neal, cofounder with wife Patricia of the Heartland Institute, which fosters social and spiritual change, notes, "When a company is spiritual, (its) practices will satisfy the needs of workers, customers, and the community. You create an organism that is stronger, more sustainable, and probably quite profitable." Companies are discovering that spiritually centered employees are the most capable of breakthrough thinking, creativity, and effective team-building and leadership. Neal adds, "Only people who are truly centered and balanced can lead business successfully in this complex environment."

Some point to Tom's of Maine as an example of a spiritually centered company. Founded by Tom Chappell, a 1991 Harvard Divinity School graduate, the company sells natural health and beauty products. Theologians are regularly brought into Tom's as guest speakers. The company also shuts down for one or two days each quarter for discussions about beliefs. A company spokesperson notes, "We don't just recognize spirituality because it's a good thing to do. It's a good business strategy. We market natural products whose benefits are less tangible. Consumers support us in part because they believe in us. The more authentic we are, the greater the return for us. We're not a product line, but a philosophy."

Another senior business leader with a sense of spirit is Lawrence Fish, chairman, president, and CEO of Citizens Financial Group, headquartered in Rhode Island. When he received his Harvard MBA, he did what no other graduating student did that year. He went to a northern India ashram and lived as ascetic for a year. Thirty years later, he still says, "There are forces that brought me to India that are still with me."

We see that in how he runs the bank. The bank's target customers are working people, not large corporate entities. Instead of eliminating people in the banking process and replacing them with ATMs, his bank has 1,500 tellers, and only about 200 ATMs. His goal is to write a thank-you note to at least one employee every day.

Before taking this job, he took a three-month sabbatical to work in a shelter for abused children. Despite the shelter director's desire to have him work on fund-raising, Fish made it perfectly clear he wasn't interested in that. "He wanted to read to children, wash walls, and be a mentor and feed the hungry," said the director.

There have been many media reports about workers who spontaneously form spiritual study groups, and about the companies that encourage and support these groups by providing the space and resources for the group to meet.

Spirituality also shows up in time away from the job. Many people are taking retreats to traditional religious sites and non-traditional facilities, such as Esalen in Big Sur. The influx has been so strong that many facilities are being stretched to meet the need. For example, the Abbey of Gethsemani in Kentucky has a one-year waiting list and the New Camaldoli Hermitage in California has a six-month wait only because they refuse to book any further out. Father Tom Gedeon of Notre Dame's Retreat International Association says that most people on retreats are baby boomers looking for answers about what to do with their life or to recharge their spirits before returning to their careers.

Your Role—Spiritual Laws to Help Transform Business

The growing spiritual awareness is changing the values and attitudes of many people in business today. The effect of these changes is already being felt in business, as the people spotlighted in this book illustrate so well.

A few spiritual laws are likely to be especially transforming for business. It is critical to note that none of the spiritual laws stands independent and apart from others. Each law actively interacts and is connected to every other law.

Try to not focus on one law at the expense of others. Focus on these laws in your personal journey in business and they will serve you well.

The Truth Is There Are Consequences

This law is known in the West as the golden rule, "Do unto others as you would have them do to you," and in the East as the law of karma (which the Bible also addresses well—"As you give, so shall you receive." [Matthew 7:12 and Luke 6:31]). The parallel to this spiritual law on the physical plane is Newton's third law of motion—for every action there is an equal and opposite reaction.

Every action we take has consequences. There are no exceptions. The intent behind the action determines the consequences. If positive intent, positive karma (or consequence) is incurred; if negative, negative karma results. The consequences of our actions are experienced either immediately or at some time in the future, which may mean in a different lifetime. (I believe reincarnation is a fact.)

As the truth and power of the law of this spiritual law is realized, managers and the rank-and-file will understand that negative actions taken will have negative consequences for them. Some will decrease their negative actions out of fear of the consequences, while others will react with other spiritual laws in mind. For example, as the unity, interconnectedness, and oneness of all is recognized, it will be a powerful moderating influence on negative actions toward others and the environment.

Check Your Ego at the Door

The second law recognizes there is a power in the universe greater, much greater, than us. For many, this recognition produces a sense of awe and humility about spirit, about God. The recognition of spirit's power humbles us all. Humility, John Templeton notes, is the gateway to knowledge and the key to progress. He goes on to define humility as ". . . understanding that God infinitely exceeds anything anyone has ever said of Him, and that He is infinitely beyond human comprehension and understanding." Templeton is the founder of a mutual fund company who now writes on spirituality.

When humbled (not weakened, but actually greatly empowered) by the power of spirit, there is a reduction in the power of the ego. As we become less self-centered and more spirit-centered, self-aggrandizing actions are replaced with actions that benefit the whole, whether it be a business team, community, a broader political entity, or the world. Winning personally will cease to be important. Instead, benefits to others move to the forefront.

This spiritual law will create a dramatic change in the business environment. While there has been more of a team approach in the last two decades, personal careers and recognition have remained the dominant and driving force behind personal actions. When people are broadly conscious of this law, true selfless teamwork will exist.

Give and Serve with a Smile in Your Heart

The third major spiritual influence on business will be the law of giving and service. The first part, giving, is only vaguely understood today. We usually see giving as good only after we satisfy all personal needs.

Giving is more than just a good idea; it is a spiritually recognized law. The Bible tells us, "It is more blessed to give than to receive" (Acts 20:35). In *The Seven Spiritual Laws of Success*, Deepak Chopra notes how giving works: "Giving engenders receiving, and receiving engenders giving." Further, he notes, "The more you give, the more you will receive, because you will keep the abundance of the universe circulating in your life."

Intent is critical in the act of giving. The intention should be to make the recipient and giver happy. Often this requires giving unconditionally. When we give without an expectation or need for gratitude, we reach the higher levels of giving.

An important form of giving is service to others. Albert Schweitzer, the noted humanitarian, said, "I don't know what your destiny will be, but one thing I know: the only ones among you who will be really happy are those who have sought and found how to serve." Chopra adds, ". . . if you want joy, give joy to others; if you want love, learn to love; if you want attention and appreciation, learn to give attention and appreciation; if you want material affluence, help others become materially affluent."

In the vast majority of businesses today, acting in accordance with this law is unfathomable. Instead, the law of how much can I take from my fellow man or from another company is the active force. At its extreme, this manifests itself as greed that is more pervasive than most would like to acknowledge. The thought of serving others is anathema to most managers; they expect employees to be loyal and to serve *them.*

The emergence of managers who view themselves as coaches and as facilitators is encouraging. While a strong personal authority undercurrent is still evident, more and more managers believe they should help others be all they can be. These managers sense that their success is a function of the group's success.

Fortunately, this is only the beginning. The personal joy and business success that comes from serving others will make us wonder how we could have been so foolish and so blind to not see its power and benefits before. The stories of people in this book are merely the leading edge of this transformation. It is up to the rest of us to take this transformation to the next level.

Many other forces will contribute to major changes in how business operates. For example, creativity will become a much greater dynamic, positive force when we understand how it works and how to manifest creative ideas. Chapter 9 details creativity's spiritual connection. The laws of detachment, intention and desire, and least effort (or as Robert Fritz popularized, the path of least resistance), and the energy of manifesting represent the science of creativity and manifesting. All these are available to us today through the works of many writers. We now need to master and harness them. When this is done, creativity will move from something that somehow happens, often unpredictably, to something we can call on at will and focus on achieving great goals.

A Spiritual Awakening—My Story

I first picked up Sanaya Roman's *Living with Joy* during a visit to a New Age bookstore in the early 1980s. I looked at it briefly, but it stayed with me as I examined more books and materials in the bookstore. This book was for me.

I have since read and reread this book many times. Each time is like the first time, as I discover new meanings that propel my life down a spiritual path. This is a very simple, yet profound book. For the first time, I experienced a deep sense of resonance and inner knowing that what I was reading was truth.

The most important lesson this book taught me was that I was responsible for and created my reality. In short, I have complete control over whether I am happy, unhappy, successful, or any other feeling that is important to me. Instead of giving power to others, I bring the power into myself. It took many years to fully integrate this lesson into my life.

Over the ensuing years, I encountered many transforming and profound books. These books include ones from Deepak Chopra, Wayne Dyer, Gary Zukav, and Stephen Covey, about such diverse subjects as quantum physics, healing, and channeled information.

While all of these have been very helpful, there are three milestones along my path. First, I discovered the 24 volumes of the Ageless Wisdom. The revelation in these more than 10,000 pages is profound and explains much of what we do not understand today about our world. The source is a master of wisdom, a Tibetan, who offers the information with no desire to convince anyone—it is up to each person to connect or not connect with his or her sense of inner knowing.

Second, there is a saying that when the student is ready a teacher will appear. Mine is Sogyal Rinpoche, author of *The Tibetan Book of Living and Dying*. My studies with him have been some of the most important days of my life, and I am eternally grateful for his wisdom. Each day I say this prayer of thanksgiving: "Sogyal Rinpoche, thank you for coming into my life and touching my life. You let me know what a human can be. Your compassion, wisdom, and joy inspire me every day. Thank you."

Third, my searching for a daily spiritual path and practice ended when I discovered the teachings of Paramahansa Yogananda, the founder of the Self-Realization Fellowship and author of *Autobiography of a Yogi*.

While I had meditated regularly for over five years before learning of Paramahansa Yogananda, the daily practical lessons from the Fellowship led my meditation to new heights and depths. Today, two mediations form the core for each of my days.

All this transformed me from a classical type-A person into who I am today. I now have a deep reverence for spirit and all that is. The message of this book—that you can be a good, caring human being and succeed in business—is one of the key messages I am deeply committed to sharing with others.

My spiritual path began while I was an executive in business. For the first 15 years on this path, I continued to rise and prosper in this role. At a point, I knew my spiritual path would lead me in different life directions. I now live my passion of wanting to help and serve others as a writer, speaker, and personal coach.

Opening to Spirit—
Inspired by a True Story

William was astounded. He'd gone with his wife to see a psychic primarily so he could reveal the psychic as a fraud. Instead he heard the psychic sharing things about his and his wife's past that no one in the city they lived in knew about. These were not generalities. The psychic named dates, names, and places. Her accuracy and confidence in what she shared with both of them was very high. Since the session had been audiotaped, William had been able to review the session afterward. This only served to further confound him.

As a business manager, William was very analytical and logical. What he just experienced was totally out of bounds of what he understood. There was no logical explanation for what had happened. Since he relied so strongly on his logical view of the world, he had no alternative explanation for what happened. He was sure of only one thing—he had heard it with his own ears and had it recorded on tape.

Before this experience, William had spent almost no time considering the paranormal. He acknowledged that there probably was a God, but his acknowledgment was unenthusiastic. And psychics were considered frauds and part of the entertainment industry.

Instead, this chance encounter inspired William to explore a world he did not understand.

Over the next several years, William became an enthusiastic and energetic explorer. He read books and met with several people who channeled information. William did not focus on the apparent magic of channeling. Rather, he focused on the substantive information he received.

William's previously unenthusiastic acknowledgment of God was now a very enthusiastic one. He used a variety of words, like universe and spirit, as synonyms for God. He also studied the links between quantum physics and God, which placated his analytical, logical mind.

Everything he learned contributed to William becoming calmer and happier. At work, he became far more receptive to different ways of looking at things. As a manager, he gave people more freedom. Increasingly, he became less concerned about being personally right. Instead, his focus was on doing what was right, even if that meant it was counter to what he previously thought.

People who had known William for many years often commented about how much he had changed. They observed that he seemed to be calmer and happier. He was easier to be around because he was a much better listener. He displayed genuine interest in new subjects, and clearly was enjoying the learning process. His business career eventually changed, but in a way that was more congruent with his evolving spiritual awareness.

Will Raap, Founder and President of Gardener's Supply, a Leading Mail-Order Garden Supply Company

For Will Raap business has two balance sheets. The first one is financial—profits, cash flow, assets, etc. The second one flows from a broader vision of his business: "If you looked at our balance sheet, you'd say 'Yeah, we're still in business after 15 years and we're moderately successful,' I suppose, but there is another balance sheet that we always try to look at; that is, the effect we have on the people who work here, on our customers, the community we're living in."

"We started from a larger context than most businesses started from," says Will. "We want to sustain ourselves as a business and financial entity, but we also want to have certain impacts on the stakeholders of the business—customers, employees, the community we're in, and the broader world." He adds, "Your livelihood needs to contribute in some meaningful and useful way to the world working better."

The business he chose enables him to make a meaningful contribution to making "the world work better." Gardener's Supply is mainly a mail-order garden supply business (there is a retail store at headquarters in Burlington, Vermont) that focuses on traditional aids to gardening, with a strong focus on organic gardening. For Will, Gardener's Supply is ". . . a company passionately committed to gardening, and its belief that gardening is a powerful force for improving the global health of the planet and its inhabitants." A company brochure amplifies on his passion: "In the garden, people come together with nature in profound and wonderful ways. As we plant, we make our world more beautiful. We learn to bring forth food and flowers where once there were none. We gain respect for the earth and our role as her steward. And we find that gardening calms the mind, steadies the heart, and elevates the spirit."

Will's spirituality is not seen in his church-going practices or his occasional meditation practice. Craig Neal, a close friend, notes, "He is spirit. His spirit manifests through his company— its values, products, and his people."

Will's strong spiritual values can be traced to several strong influences from his younger years. He received his undergraduate degree in economics from the University of California at Davis, one of the UC system's most agriculturally focused schools, and a master's degree in business and urban planning from the University of California at Berkeley in the 1960s. Berkeley in the 1960s was in part known as a center of new thinking and of challenging the status quo. Will recalls an important lesson from this time: "We have the responsibility as thinking beings to question what is true and important in a philosophical, spiritual, and political sense."

After graduation, he embarked on a career in urban planning. He quickly became disillusioned by how much short-term thinking, plus political and developer influence, controlled the planning process. His concerns about the "juggernaut of human impact on the planet" were given scant attention.

After some study about innovative planning methods, he discovered the United Kingdom was a fertile area of new thinking. He spent a summer there exploring three influences.

The first influence was a hot new book at the time, British economist E. F. Schumacher's *Small Is Beautiful* (1973). Schumacher warned that modern technology could threaten our quality of life, including our chance for justice and the opportunity for individual creativity. He argued that the earth has limited resources and that we should control growth. In addition, we should use technology to aid the renewal of natural resources. For Will, a key message was that size affects our sense of community and wholeness, a message "that resonated with me."

The second influence was the green belt and garden city approach in the U.K. This effort consciously looked at how to protect the landscape around cities. There was also a new city idea with a garden base.

The third influence may have been the most profound. He read a book about Scotland's Findhorn, described as ". . . an international community based on spiritual values, a center of adult education, and a demonstration ecological village." A two-week visit there turned into an 18-month stay. Will describes it as ". . . a place in the 70s where people came together to live lightly on the land, live harmoniously with each other, and try to create a culture that was positive in its impact."

One of the first lessons he learned was "how people could embrace high ideals and employ them in everyday life—at work or in a community context. There was a strong emphasis on understanding man's relationship to nature." We can see today how that lesson has influenced much of what he has done and is doing today.

Findhorn was a coming together of many wisdom and religious traditions, including theosophy, a significant influence for Will. According to the dictionary, theosophy is a system "purporting to furnish knowledge of God, and of the universe in relation to God, by means of direct mystical intuition, philosophical inquiry, or both." It has its roots in many Eastern and Western spiritual and wisdom traditions.

Will was also intrigued by the common threads among wisdom and spiritual traditions. When he went to Findhorn, he "wanted to find the place East and West merged, the perennial wisdom, the common bond that imbues all great spiritual traditions." This understanding provided him with a strong inner sense of the role of spirit in life. For Will, spirituality and the environment were inseparable and came together strongly in one resolutely held vision about the role of business in our world.

Today, the vision and his spiritual foundation are seen not only in the type of business Will runs, but also in the way he manages it. "One of the key issues is how to be respectful and cultivate the unique strengths and abilities of other people in the business," says Will. "We have a range of skill bases with the people who work here. The attraction was in the good measures we used in setting ourselves up in business; that is, trying to have an impact beyond the normal financial return. We attracted people who were interested in that. We needed to accommodate their unique skills and abilities. Oftentimes, we got into trouble from a financial return standpoint in doing that, but we have succeeded on the nonfinancial side."

A good example of this management approach is seen in Cindy Turcot's career. She began her career at Gardener's Supply working on computer projects. Over the years, she discovered needs and opportunities and took the initiative to address them. She improved the way customer calls were answered, responded to customer questions, handled accounts payable, established budgets, and ran human relations. Today she is both the CFO and human relations manager. Will asked her to run the financial operations because "Will wanted a *human* finance person and felt I had that. He wanted someone who was more than the bottom line."

Will has been a good role model for being a "human finance person." Early on when the company was struggling, Will wanted to give Cindy a raise, but cash flow and budgets did not seem to make that possible. Will solved it by giving her a raise and reducing his salary by an equal amount. More recently, when profits were lower than expected one year, the formula used to calculate employee bonuses did not produce an amount that Cindy thought was fair. Since the shortfall was the function of a costly computer conversion, and not the hard work of the employees, Cindy recommended higher bonuses. Will readily agreed.

Will accompanies bonus checks with a personal note thanking key managers for their specific contributions during the year. The notes have been important for Cindy, "I can't think of something nicer that a person could have said to me," she says. "It really means a lot."

Will and Cindy practice open-book management discussed in Chapter 3. Employees are stockholders, and they get complete financial disclosure. Will has strong respect for his employee stockholders.

Although he controls over 70 percent of the stock, he often respects the wishes of key managers over his desires. A few years ago, key managers were not supportive of Will's desire to expand the retail store. As president, he could have spent the $20,000 for the expansion; instead, he used his personal funds to pay for the expansion. When it quickly proved to be a financial success, the same group of key managers agreed to have the company pay Will back.

Gardener's Supply has prospered. Sales of $24.4 million in 1996 are expected to grow to about $39 million in 1999. This growth of more than 50 percent has benefited all the employee stockowners.

Through Will's enlightened management approach, employees who take a strong interest in a project often are strongly supported by him. The first example involves the Intervale, the flood plain of the Winooski River in Burlington. For centuries, it had been a fertile agricultural area farmed by early Native Americans and settlers, including Ethan Allen, a Vermont hero. Unfortunately, over the years it degenerated into a waste dumping ground and undesirable area.

Early in Gardener's Supply life, Will's urban planning vision and skill produced ideas on how to regenerate the Intervale area. He convinced the one remaining farm owner to lease him five acres to locate his company headquarters there. Besides having his catalogue business, Will saw an opportunity for composting to revitalize the Intervale soil and return it to a thriving, growing area.

Will describes the key role played by "an employee who was smitten by what we were trying to do. He had much more of an interest in the new business than what he was doing in Gardeners' Supply. So we carved out an opening in the spirit of intrapreneurship—in a business you allow businesses to emerge. We did this but not with much focus on our return on investment for the core business. It was much more about our broader sense of what business is about. It was the Intervale Farm and Garden division of Gardener's Supply Company. He then separated it into a nonprofit organization called Intervale Foundation. A couple of employees joined the organization, since it better reflected what turned them on—the nonprofit environment and the cultivation of the land resource project involving the composting effort. We discovered that we put several hundred thousand dollars of our company's money into this exercise, which was done because we had employees who could add significant value to this opportunity, by leveraging the company's investment and their own inspiration."

Today, the Intervale is the site of over 125 thriving community farms and gardens and a composting business. The entire project serves as a model for similar efforts in communities around the country.

A second example is Living Technologies. Now a separate company, it started as an effort within Gardener's Supply. The idea started with their proprietary greenhouse technology (glazing technique that has high light transmission and highly energy efficient). Again, a highly interested employee got involved.

Will describes what happened next, "We merged our greenhouse technology with his biological systems intelligence. We began ecological designed wastewater treatment systems. We have 20 to 30 of them in many countries. It is a different way of looking at sewage treatment. It is not adding chlorine and other chemicals. Instead, it becomes a biological system, much more like a garden. You manage it as an aquatic system. You bring in fish, bugs, snails, and plants to create a constructed wetland. This grew out of an individual who was excited about moving in this direction, and our willingness to see our mission much more broadly than selling gardening stuff to home gardeners. Instead, we employ the idea of gardening and the tools of gardening in a way that can effect the world in a positive way. This took about a half a million dollars from Gardener's Supply. Now we have created a separate organization and Gardener's Supply owns a minority interest. It employs 15 to 20 people today."

In the future, this exciting approach will focus on developing nations that cannot afford larger, much more expensive systems. The idea has proven economically viable in industrial applications, and should be very helpful to countries that need low-cost, sanitary methods of handling wastewater.

Outside business, Will's spirituality is seen in how he and his wife have chosen to educate their children. With other families, they founded a Waldorf school, based on the teachings of Austrian philosopher and scientist Rudolf Steiner, who also founded a spiritual movement called anthroposophy. Steiner believed that with proper development, we could access our spiritual selves with a carefully developed intellect. This spiritual capacity, Steiner believed, had been repressed by man's devotion to materialism. The practice of meditation and concentration could develop one's spiritual abilities. The Burlington school Will and others founded is now thriving.

Will Raap is that unique combination of a person with a grand vision and ability to bring the vision to life. Craig Neal considers Raap to be "one of the great visionaries and actualizers in the whole area of business and the environment, plus business and social structures." As a founder of the Heartland Institute, which is dedicated to exploring the role of spirit in business, Neal is no stranger to success or to leadership.

Craig reflects on the broader picture of what Will has accomplished so far, "From the 1950s to now, the dominant ethos has not been the common good, but really about making it in the material world. There is no shortage of heroes who have made a large profit in the material world. I think the new heroes are going to be guys like Will Raap. They have figured out mastery in the material world, but also have a much stronger vision for what the common good is all about. The mystery of what business is all about is really about serving the common good."

Looking into the future Craig observes, "Our future leaders are going to come from people with a much broader perspective, who open their hearts as well as their minds, who are balanced in body and spirit." It is great to know that we have a great start on this future in the example of Will Raap, a man who lives his spirit.

Concluding Thoughts

I believe Craig Neal is right when he says that Will Raap is the model that will become the future business hero. As spirit becomes an increasing part of consciousness, we become cognizant of business purposes beyond the traditional financial ones.

Will is a wonderful example of a person who thinks globally and acts locally. He has made a lasting impact on Burlington, Vermont, with the Intervale, the Waldorf School, and his company. With his company's international reach and the contribution that Living Technologies makes to developing nations, Will is making global contributions. I sense that there is much more that we will see from him, and projects already in the pipeline confirm this.

For a chapter on spirit, I might have included someone with a strong religious orientation, a manifestation of spirit most people are familiar with. I chose Will because his life is all about spirit. There is not much ritual associated with his experience of spirit. It is something he lives.

His spiritual perspective is an increasingly common one. It is a blend of influences that profoundly shape his beliefs about life. As people like Deepak Chopra become respected teachers, we see the benefits of blending Eastern and Western perspectives to craft a broad and inclusive view of life.

This is a major trend that is only in its infancy today. Our future leaders will emerge with a strong spiritual foundation. Their leadership will manifest much more as a teacher than as a dynamic, controlling leader.

I am fascinated that a consistent lesson of history is that change happens all the time. It happens in cycles, but it happens. At any point in time, the major influences of the near future are here now. Often they are obscure or if visible, some people ridicule them because they feel them as profound threats to their status quo.

The term New Age has been overused, misapplied, and misunderstood. Nonetheless, we are in the early stages of a new age where spirit permeates consciousness and guides us along the evolutionary path. That path leads to the unlocking of new abilities and experiences. All of them have the love and joy we so desperately seek and hunger for today.

8

INTUITION

Intuition, the most powerful form of knowing that most of us can experience, is a bit of a mystery. Many people have a deep sense that it exists and that it is very powerful. But it is as elusive as it is powerful. Defining intuition is a challenge, and describing how to invoke it is even tougher.

Since writing clear and accurate words describing intuition can be difficult, this chapter relies greatly on the words of a variety of people who clearly know what intuition is.

Intuition—A Definition

A traditional definition comes from the Swiss psychologist Carl Jung, who described intuition as one of the four major faculties of the psyche, along with thinking, feeling, and sensation. But this traditional definition is only part of the story and is somewhat misleading.

We start our exploration of intuition by acknowledging that it is an ability distinct from other human abilities, like reasoning, and that it adds value to human life. Intuition is part of a series of higher-mind abilities, higher than reasoning—abilities that are slowly being revealed to us.

Benjamin Hoff gives a wonderful introduction to intuition in *The Tao of Pooh:*

> The masters of life know the Way. They listen to the voice within them, the voice of wisdom and simplicity, the voice that reasons beyond cleverness and knows beyond knowledge. That voice is not just the power and property of a few, but has been given to everyone.

You might question whether intuition is given to everyone, but reflect for a moment on what you already know. For example, many people are frequently amazed that they seem to be able to "read the mind" of another person. Others, especially closely connected people like mothers and daughters, can sense what is happening to each other, even if the other person is a considerable distance away. This is especially true of a traumatic event that involves intense energy.

For those who are skeptical about mind reading, consider that thoughts are energy and that others can sense that energy. It is analogous to radio and television energy waves moving through the atmosphere and then being "captured" by an antenna. With thoughts, the "antenna" is our mind. For most of us that "antenna" is not operational yet, but it can be.

An important dimension of intuition, as a higher-mind ability, is that it is an inner experience. This distinguishes intuition from reasoning, which occurs partly in the inner mind—

ruminating and contemplating, for example—and partly out-side the mind—senses of touch and taste, for example.

Intuition is clear knowing arrived at without the use of facts or our logical powers. Unlike our logical mind, which is fallible, our intuition is always right, not only for us, but also for others. In addition, unlike the logical mind, intuition works swiftly, usually providing instantaneous answers to the toughest questions. Whew! That is powerful.

Intuition addresses different subjects than reasoning does. Intuition is not something we typically use to solve a com-mon mathematical problem, for example. The Ageless Wis-dom says intuition is the source of revelation that comes through an actual influx of energy, very similar to light energy. Some definitions describe intuition as the light of the soul. It is interesting to see how our language already recognizes this. For example, when we receive a revelation from our intuition we might describe it "as if a light went on" or "all of a sudden I saw the light."

At its highest levels, intuition shows ways in which human-ity can cooperate to hasten its spiritual evolution, and it reveals the spiritual laws that govern all of life. These understandings and laws are always present, but most of us are unaware of this wisdom until our soul inspires us. The soul inspires us in the di-rection of man's highest good.

While the intuition reveals "the ways of God," intuition can benefit a person regardless of whether he or she is on a conscious spiritual path, part of a religious organization, or even a believer. There is evidence, however, that having a spiri-tual, not necessarily religious, interest aids the development of the intuition's full potential.

For most people, understanding our soul is more elusive and difficult than understanding our intuition. Our soul is immortal—that quality alone tends to boggle most minds. When we are strongly identified with our personality and see-ing the world through our five senses, it is difficult to know that we have a soul. Yet, as we loosen our fixation on our outer world and start to become aware of our inner world during moments of quiet reflection, awareness gradually emerges. We experience hunches and quiet insights. As we learn to follow and trust them, we get more. Hunches eventually grow into direct, needed insights that guide us to win-win actions.

The soul and intuition are different but very connected. The wisdom traditions tell us that our intuition is the voice of our soul. In *Conversations with God, Book 2,* God says, "If you listen to your soul you will know what is 'best' for you, because what is best for you is what is true for you."

It is important to distinguish intuition from emotional desires or rational deductions. When we experience intuition, there is a deep sense of knowing, of certainty. An inner peace accompanies this sense. Intuition's guidance produces win-win solutions. When followed, the guidance tends to unfold almost effortlessly.

Another way of understanding intuition is to read the words of people who clearly used intuition in their life. Here is the 19th-century philosopher-poet Nietzsche's description of intuition:

> That which happens can only be termed revelation, that is to say, that suddenly, with unutterable certainty and delicacy, something becomes visible and audible and shakes and rends one to the depths of one's being. One hears, one does not seek; one takes; one does not ask who it is that gives; like lightning a thought flashes out, out of necessity, complete in form—I have never needed to choose. It is a rapture, the enormous excitement of which sometimes finds relief in a storm of tears; a state of being entirely outside oneself with the clearest consciousness of fine shivering and a rustling through one's being right down to the tips of one's toes; a depth of joy in which all that is most painful and gloomy does not act as a contrast

but as a condition for it, as though demanded, as a necessary color in such a flood of light. . . . Everything happens in the highest degree involuntarily, as in a storm of feeling of freedom, of power, of divinity.

In his unique manner, Nietzsche captures in words the wondrous experience of intuition that is so difficult to describe. In part, this difficulty comes from the inadequacy of our vocabulary, which struggles to describe our most spiritual or mystical experiences.

Your Role—Developing Intuition in the Business World

Everything you have read about intuition so far is from a spiritual and wisdom perspective. This perspective is the most thorough and comprehensive one we have today about our intuition.

But how does the spiritual and wisdom perspective translate to the business world? Rather easily, is the quick answer.

Intuition is a quiet voice that answers some of our toughest questions. In business we can access our intuition by creating the conditions conducive to hearing that quiet voice. Not surprisingly, creating quiet and calmness are critical to hearing the voice of our intuition.

One of my teachers provides profound counsel in four simple words—actively calm, calmly active. We should try to be inwardly calm when we are outwardly active. At all times we should create a deep inner sense of calm. When we achieve this very difficult state, we can hear our intuition's guidance.

Being calm in a business setting can sound like an oxymoron. It need not be so. Consider the following simple things you can do to start creating an inner calmness:

- Take 15 minutes each morning and afternoon to walk outside by yourself. In the first part of the walk, actively release any tensions you have. Wayne Dyer, M.D., recommends visualizing tension being released through your fingers. There are many other methods. They all ask you to consciously release tension and visualize the act of release. For the second part of your walk, focus on the wonder of your surroundings, especially nature. If there is a budding flower, stop and observe its intricacies. Allow a sense of wonder and beauty to enter your consciousness. Smile. Now bring this experience back in the building with you and stay connected to it. When you think you have lost it, bring the picture of that flower back into your consciousness. Notice how much calmer you are.

- When in a meeting where you know your opinion will be asked for, notice your breathing. It may be short and shallow. If so, change your breathing pattern to long and deep. As you breath out, release any tension and anxiety you may have. Again, visualize its release. When your opinion is asked for, pause. It does not have to be a minute, which can seem like a long time. Even 15 seconds can create the positive energy that you need. Connect with the calmness. Smile inwardly. Respond from that calmness.

- When you face a big decision, create the calm space you need to connect with your intuition. Consciously and deliberately create a peaceful, calm space in which to consider the decision. It may mean closing the office door and not answering the phone for 30 minutes. Whatever works for you, just do it. When you have created the space, visualize letting go of any negativity. Do this with a sense of lightness, not struggle. See the negative ideas floating away. When you are noticeably calmer, connect with the decision. Ask a quiet, calm inner question. Be prepared for an instantaneous, simple answer. Also be prepared to have your emotions and logical mind to argue with the response soon after it arrives in your consciousness. Do everything possible to stay connected with the energy that brought you the simple answer. Learn to trust its guidance completely.

As you become more adept at creating calmness (and it is not easy for most of us), you will connect more and more with the quiet inner voice that is your intuition. Be patient—because you are usually changing lifelong "busyness" habits that do not change easily. Endure and have the courage to follow your inner guidance that is your intuition.

Over time you will find it leads you always to the right decision. The rightness may not always be clear. In fact, as noted earlier, it may be contradicted by your emotional and logical guidance systems.

You need to know that your intuition will always lead you to win-win solutions. It leads you to what is right for everyone involved in the decision. It always takes a long-term view. You will know it is right by the inner lightness you feel, by how it makes you smile and feel relieved. You will have a deep inner knowing that it is right. You won't always be able to explain it logically—that is OK. You won't always immediately see how to execute the intuition's advice—that's OK, too. The path will be revealed at the right time. Be alert to new ideas and resources that arrive soon after the intuitive insight. They are there to help you. Be ready for the unexpected—don't reject it when it arrives. Instead, embrace it and ask how it can help you. You will get an answer.

When you first experience it, intuition may appear to occur randomly. While it can start that way, we can develop our intuition to the point where we can call upon its guidance and rely on it to answer. We can nurture the conditions where intuition flourishes.

Take some time away from the job to focus creating the following conditions at home, which can be one of the most powerful places to nurture your intuition's development. These conditions start with quiet—quiet feelings, body, and mind. When achieved (and this is difficult to achieve), the silence becomes a great teacher.

To many who have not experienced silence as a teacher, the concept seems strange, if not ridiculous. Think about a time when you have been detached from daily noise, internal and external. This may have occurred during a hike in the woods or while fishing on a lake. In those conditions, you may have had a sense of lighter, more joyful energy, even if for a few brief moments. In the presence of that energy, the previously complex may have become clear and simple or maybe you had a fresh, uplifting insight about an aspect of your life. If so, then you are approaching the intuitive field of knowing. You are starting to experience what calmer and quieter moments enable you to connect with.

In quiet moments, we become self-aware. Self-awareness is at the heart of many spiritual practices, especially meditation, which may be the most prevalent spiritual practice. Many who have a regular meditation practice discover they have greatly enhanced intuitive abilities.

Immersing yourself in great writings can also awaken the intuition, especially if you are reading wisdom or mystical texts. As I read wisdom texts on subjects I had not previously encountered, there was a constant inner companion of deep inner knowing. It was almost as if I was rediscovering an old friend or a prized value I had long forgotten. The deep inner knowing manifested as a light, joyful inner smile. Later, I would read in *Conversations with God, Book 1* that God describes the spiritual path as a process of remembering. This deep sense of remembering and rediscovering prompts the deep inner knowing.

Others who have written about intuition suggest love is a great way to access intuition. Love connects us with our highest power. When we love, we trust, and we are open.

In the same regard, fear is the biggest blocker of our intuition, as well as all other negative feelings. We need to clear any fear and associated negative emotions if the intuition is to flow freely.

Other things that can help are relaxation exercises, imagery, an excellent nutritional program, and talking to others about their intuitive experiences. In addition, scrupulous ethics are critical to developing and trusting your intuition.

In his best-selling book, *The Seat of the Soul,* Gary Zukav suggests having the right attitude is also critical to developing the intuition: ". . . allow yourself an orientation of openness toward your life and the Universe, to approach the questions in your life with a sense of faith and trust that there is a reason for all that is happening, and that the reason, at its heart, is always compassionate and good."

Intuition—A Personal Insight

Most of my life I was very analytical and logical. For a period of my life, I even denied there was a God because His existence could not be proven. So the shift from there to becoming aware of a deep inner knowing of God's existence, which transcends anything logical in its synthesis and brilliance, was a profound one.

An awakening intuition played a pivotal role in this transformation. As I read and studied various wisdom texts, I became aware of a deep inner resonance in response to what I was reading. I sensed light and lightness. A lightness of heart, joy, and inspiration were the best words I could muster to describe the experience.

As I asked questions, I received rapid responses that had the same kind of energy experience. The answers quickly proved to be right for me and everyone involved. I listened and acted on the responses. A joyous experience provided me with guidance I needed to embark on a conscious path of spiritual growth. Increasingly, I had the courage to do what my ego-guided actions would have found difficult. But is was a different kind of courage because it was easy, effortless.

Having said that, I now trust my intuition more than my logical mind trusts that 1 + 1 = 2.

In this regard, a quote from the great Tibetan Buddhist master Dilgo Khyentse Rinpoche is memorable: "The more and more you listen, the more and more you hear; the more and more you hear, the deeper and deeper your understanding becomes."

Uses and Power of Intuition

Earlier we alluded to the power of the intuition. It is ultimately the power to change the world for the better. At the highest levels, intuition works to reveal truths to benefit humanity—a power well beyond reasoning's abilities.

As we will see in Chapter 9, there is a strong link between intuition and creativity. As a result, a well-developed intuition serves the generation of new ideas and material forms to serve the planet.

Frances Vaughan, Ph.D., past president of the Association for Transpersonal Psychology and the author of the book *Awakening Intuition,* notes the contributions made in mathematics and how that occurs:

> Einstein is well known for his use of intuition, and he wrote about it also, and acknowledged that that was a very important part of his work. And mathematicians have appreciated the fact that intuition is the function that really breaks new ground, and that then logic and reason have to follow up on the intuition for proof and validation. But that creative leap is always an intuitive leap that

enables us to see things that we haven't noticed before. It's a new perception. It's as though it allows us to notice what we haven't noticed and acknowledge what we perhaps already know but have forgotten in some way.

Another notable example is Jonas Salk, the scientist who developed the cure for polio, who noted that the intuitive mind tells the thinking mind where to look next.

Intuition's power is not limited to science. It functions in every aspect of human activity, including business. Intuition will eventually grow in our lives to a point that it supersedes reason as our primary form of knowing. The Ageless Wisdom points out intuition's future role: ". . . in due time the intuition will supersede the mind, and direct spiritual perception will take the place of mental perception. . . ."

Intuitive Transformation— Inspired by a True Story

Throughout her college and high school years, Kathy had been a wizard with numbers. She received As in all the math courses she took.

When she entered business, she naturally gravitated to analyzing the results of her sales territory. When her boss worked with her, she clearly articulated every important trend in her business. Her sales presentations used many numbers, but they were always presented in a simple, easy-to-understand manner. Her buyers were always impressed by how much she knew about her business and their business. Her analytical prowess was most evident in the major presentations she made to her customers' senior management. Because she understood the business, she made a number of breakthrough sales. Not surprisingly, Kathy consistently exceeded her quotas and was promoted three times in her first five years with the company.

As Kathy's career progressed, her analytical skills served her well at every job level. Her logical and analytical abilities dominated how she looked at and evaluated the world.

During her time as a midlevel manager, some of Kathy's friends introduced her to meditation. In the beginning, it was just one of many new ideas that Kathy experimented with. She would meditate about 10 to 15 minutes on most days and found it very refreshing. It felt good and her logical mind told her it was good relaxation. It got to a point where if Kathy missed a few days of meditation she found that she felt the loss of this special time. As time went on, she meditated about 20 minutes a day on most days. About the only time she missed was when she was traveling on business.

After she had been meditating about a year, an old college friend visited her. They had not seen each other in about three years. Her friend, Allison, immediately noticed how much calmer Kathy appeared to be. Alison also noted that Kathy appeared to be more friendly and open. When Kathy heard this, she was surprised. Alison had known her well over the years and Kathy respected her views.

After Alison left, Kathy reflected on what she said. Her analytical mind wanted to know if this was the truth. She looked back over the last year after one of her morning meditations, and she realized that there had been a significant change.

Over the next several years, Kathy started to read a variety of wisdom texts and metaphysical books. She discovered something that was quite strange to her. As she read these books, she had a deep inner sense that what she was reading was right and the truth. This was a strange experience because she arrived at this conclusion without the benefit of her analytical mind. Eventually she read a book about intuition and realized that she was already experiencing intuition. This fascinated her and led to additional study.

She gradually discovered that she was bringing her intuition into the process of making business decisions. Previously when she heard a new idea, she would ask a series of analytical questions to determine whether the idea was good or not. The people who worked for her expected this and were prepared with a variety of charts and tables.

Kathy now found herself attempting to quiet her inner chatter before a meeting. She recognized that being calm and quiet was critical for her intuition to work. After a presentation had been made, she would reflect quietly for a few moments. For the people who had worked for her for many years, this was initially a bit unsettling. It was a major change from the almost machine-gun like series of questions they were accustomed to.

Kathy used this quiet moment to connect with her intuition. It provided her with broad insights about the idea, including a clear sense of what the right next steps were. Now her first series of comments and feedback provided an overview of her thinking. While she might then move to a couple of analytical questions, they were not the focal point of her reaction as they had been in the past.

Everyone she interacted with saw this change in Kathy. Senior management found her to be less combative and more open to alternative ways of viewing something. Her peers found her more pleasant to be with and more willing to collaborate on projects. The creative artists with whom she worked were struck by how much more insightful and helpful her reactions to creative ideas were. When the creative department manager shared this with Kathy, she quickly recognized that her creative meetings had become more fun and productive.

Hal Rosenbluth, President and CEO of Rosenbluth International, a Leading Travel Agency

Rosenbluth International is second only to American Express in the travel business. Its 4,500 employees work in 27 countries and more than 1,300 locations. With its Internet site you can say that they are everywhere.

For Hal Rosenbluth, Rosenbluth International's president and CEO, intuition is his key strength. Intuition provides him something he cannot get from other skills. "One of the benefits of intuition is it is a precursor so you have time to act," he says. Intuition provides insight and guidance regarding the next steps in life. The guidance leads to win-win solutions for all the people involved in an issue. Often the solutions can be at odds with accepted thinking, as Hal experiences, "I am contrarian by nature. A lot of that comes from intuition as well." Being a contrarian is something he is proud of; he has adopted the salmon as the company mascot because of its great ability to swim upstream against great odds.

For Hal there are definite indications that his intuition is at work, "It makes my body tingle. Intuition is like a road sign." Most people with a developing intuition report a physical manifestation. It can be the tingling that he experiences, a sense of deep inner peace, or a heartfelt inner knowing that prompts a smile.

Interestingly, intuition is something that can be unnoticed in our life for many years. If asked before becoming conscious of it, we might even deny its presence. Hal had a similar experience: "I never really thought about my intuition until about five or six years ago. I am not sure that if someone is intuitive that they recognize it as such."

Yet, when he became aware of his intuition, he looked back over his life and recognized that he had probably been intuitive for many years. His first, powerful memory occurred about 30 years ago, when he was driving away from home. He had gone about 20 miles when "for some unknown reason I turned the car around." He had a deep sense of urgency: "I drove as fast as I could back home, and as soon as I got there I found my grandmother lying on our driveway." No one else had noticed her, and Hal provided immediate assistance. At the time, he recalls, "I had no idea why I did that."

The event was the first where a deep inner sense proved to be true and of great assistance for Hal. Now aware of his intuitive ability he notes, "I have had similar things like that happen in my life." He finds his intuition is an unusual skill, but one that is very valuable and increasingly trusted.

While it took him years before he recognized his intuition, it is a strength that is also obvious to others and greatly appreciated by them. Ralph Smith, who has known Hal since 1981, has seen his intuition at work, "He has empathy and the ability to read people. His antenna goes up and he is intuitive. He has a sense of when people are hurting and what he can say and do to reach people. There is no way you can teach that."

Joe Terrion, a vice president at Rosenbluth International, has seen Hal's intuition at work with people: "He is very sensitive to how people are feeling. What they are thinking and what their perspective is on a situation is important to him. People really notice that, appreciate it, and like it. He's always considering the other person's point of view. He does the same thing with associates, customers, and suppliers." Intuition helps him be an "extraordinarily good listener. He listens to hear the real message a person is trying to communicate."

We need courage to act on the insights intuition gives us, says Hal. An example of his courage to do the right thing came a few years ago with one of their largest customers. He heard that the customer was consistently being rude and abusive to his agents. He got personally involved by monitoring calls and confirmed this report. He then withdrew as a vendor to the rude customer. He notes, "Many people rolled their eyes and said 'what is he doing now?' But I could just not be a leader in a company where people were abused."

Not surprisingly, some of the people who have inspired him the most over the years also demonstrated great courage to do what was right, especially when it involved doing the previously unacceptable or unthinkable. Martin Luther King is one of his heroes. About King he recalls, "He stood up for what was right.

He put his life on the line. He motivated people. He had a vision and stuck with it, even though it was lonely and tough."

Another man of great courage was Anwar Sadat, the former president of Egypt. Hal recalls, "He went against the popular belief and paid the price of his life." Both King and Sadat paid the ultimate price for the courage to do what they deeply believed was the right thing to do.

One of the abilities of intuition is the turning what appears to be a negative time into a positive one. Joe notes this about the company's toughest time, "Our toughest time was also our one of our most spectacular moments."

The company was facing pressures on revenues as airlines reduced commissions or threatened to do so. Rosenbluth International had experienced great success with an innovative organizational design, but there were signs that it was no longer serving their needs as growth accelerated. The company operated with separate operations and client services organizations, but they were increasing at odds with each other, which hurt their ability to get as close to customers as they needed to be. In addition, two separate organizations was expensive.

This led to almost two months of study. The new plan combined both operations and client services under one general manager for a single company or similar group of companies. Many other concerns were aired before they announced the plan's implementation. When they looked back six months after implementation, they saw a nimble, fast, and client-intimate structure.

The change required a general manager to be an expert in both disciplines where they were now only skilled in one. It also meant displacing some people from current customers and temporarily having undefined assignments. Virtually every management associate in the company would have a new assignment and most of the other associates would have a new boss or customers. With this much change, Hal knew it required his most sensitive abilities.

He decided to invite all the new general managers to a three-day meeting in North Dakota, where they had a reservations operation and meeting rooms. For a Philadelphia-based company, this clearly qualified as going offsite. Joe noted the mood when people arrived, "When they arrived they were nervous, anxious. If they had been in operations they were concerned about what they did not know about client services and visa versa."

Hal gave an opening one-hour talk with almost no notes. People in attendance noted that while he was addressing one hundred people, it felt like a one-on-one discussion. He spoke from his heart and answered questions as they arose.

Over the three days of introduction and training, Hal arrived early to meetings to answer questions and stayed late after dinner to help people with any issues they had. At the conclusion of the three days, Joe noted the mood had changed dramatically. "When we left you would have thought we had won the NBA championship. We hadn't really begun implementation and people were on fire."

Not long after this change, there was another major change. Instead of making reservations in many locations, large telecenters would make most reservations. Again, there were displacements in many cities, but the people who no longer ticketed at their site transferred to other assignments in most cases. Because the move to general managers had gone so well, this move went much smoother than many expected. Hal reminded people that when they first went to computers, there was concern about layoffs. Instead, the computers and other changes enabled the company to better serve customer needs, which fueled continued dramatic growth.

Hal and Diane Peters wrote a book about the underlying philosophy of Rosenbluth International. Its title is a great theme —*The Customer Comes Second.* Number one is the associate who works at Rosenbluth.

He explains: "We believe that only if our people are first in our eyes will they be able to put the customer first in theirs. In other words, to put someone else first and mean it, you have to know what it feels like on the receiving end." In another context, he explained their approach this way, "The principle behind it is straightforward. It's our people who provide service to our clients. The highest achievable level of service comes from the heart. Therefore, the company that reaches its people's hearts will provide the very best service. It's the nicest thing we could possibly do for our *clients.* They have come to learn that by being second, they come out ahead."

He adds, "Our time on earth is finite. The majority of everyone's waking hours are spent at work. A company has an obligation to the people it employs to make that part of life pleasant and happy."

Hal uses two approaches to accomplish this objective. The first is the care he takes in hiring people, and the second is management philosophy and programs.

In hiring people, Rosenbluth is very careful and choosy— in one year the company hired 800 of 21,000 applicants. The key to hiring decisions is finding nice people. "Niceness is the essential ingredient," says Hal. "If they are nice, then we'll look at work history, skills and so forth. But we cannot teach being nice."

One way he defines "nice" is by drawing this comparison: "There's the type of person who pushes his way to the front of the line to snare a seat on the commuter train and the type of person who offers his seat to others."

The company wants people who are not afraid to try something different and work in a company that rewards people for creativity, energy, and innovation. By hiring nice people, Hal believes he can create an environment of friendship, honesty, and trust. To help him do this his intuition again plays a role, "Nice people know nice people. It is intuitive."

In hiring managers, he looks for qualities in addition to being nice, "The first is that they do not take themselves too seriously, but recognize that other people do. And second that they spend the majority of their time with our people and our clients and listening to what they have to say."

Beside hiring the right people, it is critical for management to create a culture and daily environment where people can flourish. His response to the question about what he enjoys the most about his job was, "Seeing people in our company accomplish something that maybe they never thought possible before."

Hal also looks at his job as the "executive in charge of sleep." "My role is to create an environment conducive to our people and our clients getting a good night's sleep. I think that's done by ensuring that we run an honest and ethical company, one where people can work hard during the day but then go home and not have to worry about things like bureaucracy or frustration in the workplace, whether it be internal to Rosenbluth or external as part of the client. If I'm doing my job correctly, then our people and our clients are getting a good night's sleep, and that's kind of rare these days." The result is that his priorities are "people, service, profits, in that order."

Hal helps people in a number of ways, beginning with a newly-hired person's two-day orientation and training program at the company's Philadelphia headquarters. Hal knows people are excited and motivated when they start a job. Instead of having them fill out forms, take a physical, or other administrative routines, he treats new hires royally. The two days conclude with tea being served late in the second day by Hal and other top executives. For Hal, it is an opportunity for him to learn about new people and for them to get any questions asked that they might have. He believes getting off to a great start is crucial to achieving the environment they want to have.

Along with this program, Hal has a standing offer for any associate to spend a day with him seeing what his job is about. When I conducted my first interview with him, an associate was present the entire time. He has an 800 number where any associate can call and leave a message or ask a question. Replies are prompt and many times Hal responds personally. The company periodically asks staff how they are feeling through questionnaires. Associates also have the opportunity to review Hal himself. "Since I am not the only person who likes to question the status quo, we give everyone regular opportunities to review executive performance and tell us how they would run the company," he says. "It's been a highly successful program in generating new ideas, and if constructive criticism is a gift, then in my office it tends to be Christmas every day."

The result of the good hiring decisions and management is a company that excels at providing service to its clients. They are a winner of the Tom Peters award as Service Company of the Year. Peters, author of *In Search of Excellence* and proponent of customer-driven companies, had a strong influence on Hal, but in an unusual way. He built on Peters's quality- and customer-driven ideas by determining that he would make associates number one. He knew that in competing with American Express that he could not match their considerable strengths, so he needed unique qualities. Hal's friend Ralph Smith observed, "Hal recognized that he had to do something unusual if he was going to succeed versus American Express and others. He decided to create a culture that was unusual. He created psychological benefits that made people happy working there. It is a fun place, a place where your work is appreciated."

Spectacular success has been the result of Hal's efforts. He joined the family business, founded in 1892, out of college in 1974. Sales then were less than $25 million, and they came mostly from traditional local travel agency sources—vacation travel, for example—and only 25 percent from corporate travel. Today sales are more than $3.5 billion and almost 100 percent of this comes from serving corporate clients like Wal-Mart, Merck, Intel, and Oracle. Hal led the company's conversion to serving corporate clients. Their first major client was Du Pont in 1985. The shift to corporate clients involved expanding beyond their Philadelphia base to numerous cities in the United States and to several countries.

Concluding Thoughts

Intuition is a remarkable ability. As we learned in the chapter, it is never wrong. It leads us to our higher good and others in a positive direction through its win-win solutions.

In an era where we hunger for answers and direction, we have intuition to help us. With so much power available to us to address life's most important issues, why isn't everyone signing up for classes on how to develop this amazing ability?

The answers are many but quickly fall into two groups. The first group is about doubt. We doubt intuition really exists, and if it did happen to exist, it is utterly unpredictable and untamable. The second group of answers deals with the lack of teachers and role models. Even if we open up to the possibility that intuition exists, we cannot learn about it, at least that is the hypothesis.

I hope this chapter has opened up your mind on both counts. Intuition absolutely does exist, and we can invoke and "tame" it. We can learn to be intuitive. The "classes" usually do not feature intuition in the title. You are more likely to find intuition skills taught indirectly in meditation courses. Meditation nurtures the conditions where intuition develops.

Consciously developing your intuition and experiencing its power is a wondrous experience. Intuition is one of my life's many highs. When I ask a question that I want my intuition to address, the answer usually arrives very quickly, often a nanosecond after I complete the question. For this to occur, I need to ensure the inner conditions are optimal—peace, quiet, and connection with as high a level of consciousness that I can muster at the time.

If these conditions are not present, the answer can come from a variety of sources—emotional, logical, and physical. Each of these sources has its telltale signs. For example, an emotional answer has sensations associated with my gut or third chakra area. The energy sensations are more intense and maybe with a tinge of fear. This is very different from the intuition's sensations that have calm, almost soft energy and there is a sense of knowing the answer is right. And it is.

The challenges I face with intuitive messages are learning to trust the message, and then not distorting it by putting it through evaluation by my emotions, logical thinking process, or physical abilities. When I act on my intuition's guidance, I center myself at as high a level of consciousness as I can achieve that moment. If not, the actions are influenced by the other evaluative systems, emotions, for example. When this happens, I inevitably redirect good direction to some degree. The change in direction, even if apparently small, can negate much of the intuition's wise counsel if I am not conscious of what is happening. If conscious, I have the opportunity to get back on track.

For Hal intuition is not something he evaluates. Instead, he knows he has it and greatly appreciates its contributions. When you see what he has created at Rosenbluth International, there is no doubt he has used higher levels of perception and evaluation to show the way along his path.

For Hal there is no conscious spiritual connection with his intuition. He can feel it in his body—a pleasant tingle—and trusts its guidance. He knows it is distinct from his emotions and logical thinking abilities. It is the strongest skill he uses to manage the business.

While he has been consciously aware of his intuition and called it that for less than ten years, he knows it has been with him far longer than that. Now that he is conscious of it, intuition takes on an ever-increasing role. It will be fascinating to see where it leads.

9

CREATIVITY

*Assume that fairly well-developed people
would rather create than destroy.*

· · · · ·

—One of Abraham Maslow's keys to enlightened
management, *Maslow on Management*

There is broad consensus that creativity is a valuable business skill. It produces new solutions to old problems and inventions that better serve the needs of customers, for example. While there is broad agreement about its value, fully understanding creativity is a somewhat elusive endeavor.

We tend to judge some people as creative and others as not creative. This is a dangerous myth, because it eliminates many wondrous sources of creativity. We are all creative—capable of looking at material forms or ideas and seeing new possibilities. While each person is capable of different levels of creativity (all of us may not have the creativity of John Lennon and Paul McCartney, for example), once we accept that everyone is creative, we will be positively surprised much more than we will be disappointed.

Some people view creativity as a skill that is difficult, if not impossible, to invoke when and where we need it. This view holds that creativity is random or unpredictable. When we understand how creativity works, we quickly realize there is a proven creative process and conditions where creativity flourishes. While most of us may not be capable of snapping our fingers and being creative, we can learn to begin the creative flow if we are willing to be patient for as little as five minutes. With these understandings, we can quickly see how creativity becomes an exceptionally valuable skill to use in the achievement of wise success.

In the following sections, creativity is defined from a wisdom perspective. Next I discuss ways to access it when and where it is needed, and then discuss ways to best manifest a creative idea.

Defining Creativity

There is a close connection between intuition and creativity. In his book, *The Seat of the Soul,* Gary Zukav says, "Intuition serves creativity." The higher mind, of which intuition is a part, is directly involved in the creative process.

Creativity brings something into being that did not exactly exist previously. Creativity can result in minor modifications or in never-before-seen ideas or material forms.

Creativity manifests itself in a wide range of ways. Thinkers of all kinds have dissected the levels and types of creativity. The number of types and levels ranges from two to more than ten.

Creativity—The Wisdom Connection

The Ageless Wisdom highlights creativity's spiritual connection: "Creative work proves the fact of the soul . . ." and then defines how this is accomplished: "Through the use of the creative imagination, the soul creates; . . ." It goes on to note: "The more advanced the person, the more the soul is the person, the more you are really seeing the nature of that person's soul, and the more creative that person becomes; . . ."

We do not have to be conscious of the soul's influence for creativity to function in the manner just described. Creativity can flourish in a person who is not conscious of the soul's influence when there is a strong ethical foundation, for example.

Your Role—The Creative Flow

In an inspiring passage, the Ageless Wisdom notes that creativity works through "the cultivation of the creative imagination." It goes on to say the following:

As yet, humanity knows little about this faculty, latent in all men. A flash of light breaks through to the aspiring mind; a sense of unveiled splendour for a moment sweeps through the aspirant, tensed for revelation; a sudden realization of a colour, a beauty, a wisdom and a glory beyond words breaks out before the attuned consciousness of the artist, in a high moment of applied attention, and life is then seen for a second as it essentially is.

In this moment of realization, life is wondrous and effortless; life is full of light. Even as that moment regrettably slips away, we can recapture some, most, or all of the vision, if we know the creative process.

To recapture the vision, we need to do three things. First, we need to persevere. Second, we need to hold as high a point of consciousness as possible; meditation is very helpful here. Third, we need to focus our creative imagination on as much of the revelation as we can. This picture-making function links the mind and brain (which are distinctly different entities). When we make the link, we can start the process of bringing the revelation from inside to outside as notes, pictures, sounds, or other appropriate manifestations. There can be a sorting out and assembling process as we recall the various parts of the revelation.

While much of what has been said about the process of creativity may seem to apply to great creative achievements, the principles apply at every level of creativity. Even if we are trying to fix a malfunctioning bicycle, we can have a flash of inspired thought that reveals the solution. Our challenge then becomes how to fully capture the inspiration and translate it into using the right tools in the right way.

This experience of creativity works in every aspect of life, including business. The breakthroughs in business are the result of creative insight. When you are conscious and aware of the creative process, you retain more of the creative insights. When creativity flows, you know how to stay connected to the creative flow. Your awareness is acute and focused. This can be difficult in some business situations, but as your creative skills grow, you learn how to stay connected in even the most trying of circumstances. Recall how, in Chapter 8, the value of being actively calm and calmly active was articulated. This same awareness and skill play a major role in enabling creativity to flow.

To optimize creativity, certain elements must be in place: The mind must be quieted, just as is the case when accessing intuition. The best way to do this is by meditating. If that is not possible or acceptable, then getting into a quiet external environment or relaxing in nature helps. When the external environment is quiet, then it is possible to let go of as many thoughts as possible. If these thoughts involve negative emotions like fear or anxiety, it is especially critical that we find a way to release them. Easily said, but clearly this can be a challenge.

With a quiet mind we then can embark on developing additional conditions for creativity to succeed. The following is out of necessity only a partial list, and anyone wanting to know more can find more conditions from many books on the subject, as well as from creative consultants.

Again, in business it can sometimes be difficult to produce the calmness. Thus, it is not surprising to hear many business-people relate how they came up with a creative insight in the shower or while running.

The more you understand the optimal conditions for creativity, the more you can purposefully bring them into your life. Often it is easiest to begin the effort away from business. But gradually you learn how to bring them into your time at work.

Creativity does not only happen during quiet times, as Doug Hall knows. Doug is the founder and CEO of Richard Saunders International (RSI), a Cincinnati-based think tank of professional strategic inventors that help companies invent new products and business strategies. He recommends adding lots of visual stimulation and "mixed, diverse brains" to the creative process. He gives the following illustration: If you sit down with a writing pad to brainstorm vacation ideas, you would drain your brain of ideas in maybe a page. Now, if you add to the process numerous travel brochures, your list of ideas doubles or triples in size. Finally, now invite a group of world travelers who have lived in numerous countries, and your list of ideas again doubles or triples in size. By involving people with diverse experiences, you tap into a powerful resource. This is why Doug involves accountants, musicians, poets, and DJs, for example, in his idea-generating sessions for clients trying to develop new consumer product ideas, like new iced-tea concepts.

Doug's approach is a proven winner with businesses. Many of the big names in marketing use Doug and his company to help generate new ideas.

His approach also works on a smaller scale within a business. Some of the steps you can take to use his ideas for your idea-generating session are:

- Find a fun offsite location. The best locations combine a retreat atmosphere with fun things to do during breaks. The retreat atmosphere is usually in a wonderful nature setting—paths through the woods, ponds, and flower gardens, for example. The fun can include miniature or real golf and go-kart racing.

- Invite mixed brains to your meeting—people who have a sense of fun, people from outside your business, people known for their creativity in any area—music and art, for example.
- Bring in lots of visual stimulation. Bring in product samples and copies of advertising to play on a VCR. If you are working on new exotic flavor ideas for a beverage, bring in plenty of pictures of jungles, tropical islands, and other exotic locations. Do not be limited by pictures. Bring in actual products you can use and have fun with.
- Import fun into your creative session. Bring fun into the room. Nerf guns, balls, Frisbees, and fun music all help. When you have fun, you connect to the creative flow. Creativity flows when the energy is light, not heavy, serious, and strained.

Other steps include relaxation, pampering yourself, reading an inspirational book or poem, and listening to uplifting music. Being with someone you love and expressing love to all that is around you also facilitates the creative flow. The objective of all these steps is to elevate your consciousness to as high a level as possible.

Your Role—Manifesting Creative Ideas

Once you have a creative idea, the next challenge is manifesting the idea. So many ideas stop at the idea stage, because bringing the idea to life seems to be difficult, even impossible. We drop the idea down to the level of the rational mind and emotions for evaluation. That's when judging and fears creep in and diminish the creative idea. If only we knew the "secrets" of manifesting our ideas!

There are no secrets. Many wise people have written on the manifestation process. In this section, we briefly touch on some key points and, again, there are many resources if you want to learn more.

The starting point is having a clear vision of the desired result. If you do not have the end in mind, you will quickly lose the inspiration in a sea of executional junk.

Knowing the end we seek often requires retrieving that initial revelation. As noted earlier, there is a process for recapturing the initial revelation, and it is important to follow this closely. If we start with only a vague outline of the creative revelation, the parts that are missing or incomplete may cripple the whole idea.

In business, the creative idea takes the next steps and becomes a concrete vision. Creating the vision requires staying connected to the creative flow and translating the idea into words and sometimes pictures. When the creative idea starts to take shape, a flip chart can be useful to capture free-flowing ideas. No judging of ideas is allowed—at this stage, there are no bad ideas.

Having diverged with a wide range of ideas, there comes a time to bring a modest amount of focus to the idea. A combination of group and individual effort selects the components of the vision. The balance between individual and group effort at this stage varies, but ultimately it is best if the creative owner of the idea plays an important shaping role.

With the end in mind, we are ready to manifest the idea.

There is a very practical outline of the manifestation process in *Conversations with God, Book 2:*

Thought is the first level of creation.

Next comes the word. Everything you say is a thought expressed. . . . Words are more dynamic . . . than thought, because words are a different level of vibration from thought. They disrupt . . .

Next comes action.

Actions are words moving. Words are thoughts expressed. Thoughts are ideas formed. Ideas are energies come together. Energies are forces released. Forces are elements existent. Elements are particles of God, portions of All, the stuff of everything. . . .

The process of thought-word-action involves the mind. The mind creates. The mind keeps the idea in the light of the initial revelation. Holding the light steady requires willpower and perseverance. When this is done, the idea eventually manifests in tangible outer form.

Wayne Dyer is particularly helpful in pointing out the power of the mind in manifesting intentions. "Your thoughts and visualizations are your source of manifesting. It is this energy that you want to activate and make work for you. The mental-picturing process and its application to the manifesting process are something that you can experience when you are in a state of complete faith." He adds, "The mental picturing power is the energy of attraction that is in all creative processes." His book *Manifest Your Destiny* is an excellent resource.

Leveraging the mind's powerful role in creativity helps to create tension between where we are now and where the creative idea would take us. Robert Fritz, a preeminent thinker on creativity and author of *The Path of Least Resistance,* notes the role of this tension: "In the orientation of the creative, the discrepancy between the current reality and the vision is an important dynamic, for out of that discrepancy the natural play of structural forces can be fully engaged and mobilized to bring about the results you want."

In business it is often helpful to maintain the duality between where you are now and where you will be when the idea is manifested. Keeping a group focused on this duality helps create the dynamic tension that propels them forward. Sometimes people are motivated not so much by the new idea as by wanting to change the current situation.

With vision, intent, an engaged mind, and dynamic tension established, we need to open ourselves up to the universe's help. For creativity to continue its work, we need to be focused on our intent and the vision, but we need to let the universe define the rest. This is a leap of faith most controlling people are unwilling to take. If you feel resistant, try to find an area where you are willing to let the universe handle the details. Eventually you will learn how miraculously this happens. You will know you are following the universe's path when that path is easy and joyful. If you are struggling, back up and take another path.

Some people misinterpret this to mean all we have to do is launch the intent and sit back and wait for the results to appear on our doorstep. More is required. We need to hold the vision and the intent in our consciousness, and act each day on that intent, going with the flow of "gifts" the Universe presents us to achieve our vision.

In business, this process can sometimes be a challenge. Businesses often quickly want very detailed systematic plans for how an idea will move from the concept to an actual product or program. If this is required in your company, you can create the plans and still proceed in a very open fashion. The challenge of detailed plans is that they often limit your ability to learn as you go and to adopt new and better ways of bringing the idea to life.

Creating This Book

As I embarked on writing this book, I had a very strong vision of the message I wanted to share. I wanted readers to know that they could be good human beings and be successful in the competitive business environment. This vision came to me while I was driving to our mountain home with my dog for a quiet, reflective weekend. Listening to Garrison Keillor's "Writers' Almanac" on National Public Radio, he mentioned that it was baseball player and manger Leo Durocher's birthday, and that the title of his autobiography was *Nice Guys Finish Last*. It immediately hit me that I wanted to share the message with people that *nice guys finish first*. The titled changed over time, first to the gender-neutral *nice folks finish first* and then to the current title. While titles changed the vision, the messages were steadfast.

The question then became how to bring it to life. While this question had many answers over time, there was always the light of the vision to show the way and to evaluate which of multiple approaches best communicated the message.

For example, I had a tentative plan that included several potential business leaders. Instead of being wed to the plan and list of names, I went with the flow each day. Regularly new names and resources revealed themselves, and they enriched and developed the idea. The final list of leaders has only one person who was on my original list. Chapter subjects changed as I learned more, including some that I had not previously considered. I was very in the moment, focused only on what I was doing that day or hour.

I held the vision of the book constantly in my consciousness. It guided me and made the path effortless and joyful. I had total confidence the book would be published even as I collected an impressive array of rejection letters, first from agents and then publishers. I was undeterred, but not in a bulldog sort of way. Rather, my vision and intent were crystal clear. They never wavered. I merely acted on the opportunities each moment presented to me. That's fun and effortless—no stress allowed!

Creativity Is Fun—
Inspired by a True Story

For almost five years, Henry was troubled by how the creative process worked in his company. He attended a creative meeting and was presented with a range of creative ideas. Sometimes the ideas were rejected immediately because they were not on the strategy that he asked for. When this happened, there was often a lot of tension and hard feelings, since all the work was usually scrapped. After this kind of meeting, he was not surprised to have to wait almost a month before the next creative meeting was scheduled. He guessed that part of this time was caused by the hard feelings that resulted in the creative group taking time off from the project.

Off-strategy work was the exception. In most creative meetings, Henry would have one or two favorite ideas. He would ask for more work to be done on each one of the directions that showed promise. The creative group then seemed to disappear for another two or three weeks. At the next meeting, Henry would discover either that there had been a clear understanding at the previous meeting or that there had not been. When the latter occurred, there could be more hard feelings because the creative group felt they had wasted time because of poor direction. These hard feelings seemed to inevitably lead to another three or four weeks before Henry would see the next round of creative work. When the former occurred, everyone was feeling good and any additional revisions seemed to take about a week or less.

While Henry was not allowed into the creative process, he suspected that less than four days' work was put in on the project despite the four weeks between meetings. Initially Henry did not have the answer, but his deep feeling was that the creative process could be compressed from months into days.

He began to explore how others managed the creative process. Among his best sources, he found a consistent theme.

When creativity seemed to work best, people had fun and freely collaborated.

Henry had a major project coming up where he thought he would try a new approach. He met with the head of the creative department and outlined his thinking. Henry wanted to invite a wide range of people to an offsite creative development meeting. He suggested having teams work on the same project independently for short periods. Fun needed to be built into the entire process.

The head of the creative department thought it was a great idea. His quick support for the idea was exhilarating for Henry.

Over the next few days, Henry chose a secluded site with an ocean view. He invited about 20 people with a variety of backgrounds to the two-day session. Some of these people were from outside the company and were invited because of their ability to bring fresh thinking into the mix. Two participants were in charge of creating the spirit of fun for the two-day session.

On the first day of the session, four teams of about five people each were assembled. Each team had an artist and a person who was skilled at using computer graphics programs. People with a variety of skills and backgrounds completed the teams. Each team worked independently for about 90 minutes. Some teams chose to work in the sand dunes near the beach.

When they reported back and shared their results, Henry was astounded at their results. Each team had developed highly creative ideas and had received quality feedback from the other teams. After taking a break following the presentations by the teams, Henry decided to focus on three very promising ideas. The teams went off for another couple of hours to develop these three ideas.

When they reported back, Henry was again very impressed by the quality and quantity of work done. They were now ready for the next step. That evening, they went to a pre-arranged focus group where consumers had the opportunity to react to the creative ideas. The input received from consumers was used the next day to take the ideas to even higher levels.

The schedule was leisurely and allowed for relaxation on the beach, Frisbee throwing, and a spirited flag football game.

In two days, Henry estimated that he had made two or three months' progress. After another week for final polishing and another focus group, Henry was confident enough in the creative ideas to present them to senior management.

Everyone felt good about the process, especially the creative department. The new process was used for every important project.

Cliff Einstein and Brian Morris, Dailey and Associates, a Leading Advertising Agency

Cliff Einstein and Brian Morris are a terrific team.

Cliff has a passion for creating. As creative director, it is his business to develop ideas that help clients sell more of their products. The products are diverse and include Honda motorcycles, Nestle Crunch, Callaway Golf, Robert Mondavi Winery, and Alpo.

When Cliff speaks to groups about creativity, he articulates several rules that have guided him over the years. They include the ability to "welcome your mistakes" and to "welcome your fears." Not welcoming mistakes and fear can cripple the creative process. Looked at one way, there are no mistakes, just steps along the path to creating an idea.

"Be willing to be stupid" is a great rule that opens up entirely new possibilities. This willingness frees a person of others' expectations and removes the inhibitions that can stifle creativity.

His last rule is "Don't make rules."

Cliff brings us inside the development of an ad campaign for a new account. The agency won the account for El Pollo

Loco, a fast-food chicken restaurant, and they needed a new advertising campaign. Many people developed ideas, and one day Brian asked Cliff if he had ever heard of the chicken dance. Brian had seen it at one of his son's dances. Brian remembered people had a lot of fun and that it was visually interesting.

The idea intrigued Cliff, and he decided to focus on the idea. He describes what happened next, "I have a nice little process that works for me. I get into bed and just before I go to sleep I think about it. It is very quiet, very clear, and I can get it together. Very often at five in the morning, I am up and it is cooking. I start writing, then pretty soon its flowing. I got it right away. I wrote it in 12 minutes." In the ads, unlikely people dance the chicken dance as a sign that they have gone crazy for chicken. The line is "Go to El Pollo Loco when you are crazy for chicken."

Cliff's process of planting a seed before bedtime and then harvesting the benefits in the morning is letting the universe handle the details.

Being this quick and skilled comes with over 30 years of experience. Phil Joanou, who preceded Cliff as chairman, saw his quick response to a creative problem, "He has a very unique sense of being a very smart businessman and a very creative guy. He has the ability to focus his creativity on solving a problem. He is so very, very fast, so fast you can't believe it."

Phil recalls how they won the Honda motorcycle account in competition with other agencies. At the briefing, he observed how Honda, the leader in motorcycle sales, was not taking the initiative, instead acting as if it were a distant third in the market. After the briefing Cliff and Phil returned to their offices. Very quickly thereafter, Cliff came up with the line that became the campaign theme for many years: "Follow the Leader." He followed this up with a range of ideas to fully develop all the dimensions of the idea, including a strong musical theme. Honda has remained an account for more than 15 years.

Cliff is a skilled professional creative who demonstrates that creativity is a developed skill. His peers have recognized the brilliance of his work many times. His awards include a CLIO, an International Broadcasting Award, an *Advertising Age* Magazine Award for best TV ad, and the Award for Best Advertising Campaign in America by the American Advertising Federation.

While Cliff is a top creative talent today, when he started out in life he stood a greater chance of becoming a performer, actor, or comedian then the head of a large agency. His father set the tone, "He was very fast, witty, and sharp, very astute with a tremendous sense of balance and dignity." His father started in advertising with a chain of furniture stores in Boston. For the advertising, he created a character, Parkyakarkus, a funny Greek. Eddie Kantor, a famous comedian of the time, heard about the ads and told Cliff's father he should be in entertainment. He started on Kantor's radio show and then went into show business.

The show business background drew Cliff's two brothers. Albert Brooks is one brother who has appeared in many movies, and his other brother, Dave, is a two-time Emmy winner.

Cliff went through high school without a clear idea of what he wanted to do. He showed leadership qualities as student body president in high school. He graduated from UCLA with a BA in English in 1961. About this time, a fraternity brother from college invited Cliff to go with him to a seminar put on by the Success Motivation Institute. His friend was in real estate sales, and had to use his strongest persuasive powers to convince Cliff to attend.

At the seminar speaker's request, Cliff wrote down a long-term goal and then the speaker instructed him to write down a number of short-term goals. Having completed that, the speaker advised, "If the short-term goals line up and feed the long-term goal, you're happening. It is going to be all great. If they don't, you're in trouble. You will zigzag all around, knocking off all these short-term goals, but they won't be leading to the long-term goal. You will waste a lot of time and energy. You will not get what you want to get."

The process made sense, so when Cliff went home, he dedicated himself to finding a goal. At first it was "I want to be really good at what I do." He recognized this was too vague. When he reflected on what he really loved to do, he knew he wanted to find a way to combine his love of writing and creativity. He updated and adjusted the general goal through the years to target specific levels of achievement.

He also wanted to distinguish himself in the family. Since his two brothers were entertainers, especially comedy, he decided he would be the culture brother. Ultimately, this focus led to becoming a leading art collector (listed as one of the top 100 collectors in America) and a trustee of the Museum of Contemporary Art.

Cliff feels the early goal-setting process served him well.

In 1965, Cliff cofounded Silverman/Einstein, a new product development company, which was later sold to Interpublic. In 1968, he joined Peter Dailey and others to form Dailey and Associates. When Dailey was eventually sold to Interpublic, Cliff made enough money to consider other career paths. Over the next several years, he produced a play in Los Angeles and San Francisco, worked on a comedy show as a rewrite person *(The Last Resort)*, started a furniture import business with furniture from Milan, started a little bank with others, and did the main titles for a network show called the *Six O'clock Follies*.

Despite this flurry of activity, he realized, "I wasn't as good at any of those things as I was at advertising. So I returned my high energy back to advertising."

Cliff is a dynamic and passionate person. Joe Murray, who works with him as a director of commercials, observes, "He has a genuine joy and enthusiasm. He is a joyful man." Joe believes his passion allows him to not fear failure, "Cliff is not afraid of failing. He knows what he wants. He is always willing to take a chance. He is willing to try something new, a little off center. He is very, very fresh."

Sometimes passionate people can be flighty. Not Cliff. Phil Joanou sees him as a deeply committed person, "He stays committed to stuff in an age where it is easy to jump around for the next buck. There is real loyalty and commitment." He adds, "When he gets into something, he really commits to doing it right."

Cliff seems to love his work. "At this point in my life, I am folding in all my interests in travel and visual culture into the atmosphere that we work in, which then comes back out in better advertising. This gives clients more confidence, and makes our people want to work here more. I have created a sort of theater of life to perform in, and I am the producer. It is very fulfilling for me and makes me want to keep coming back to work."

Brian Morris could have been very successful in the creative area had he turned his talents in that direction. Instead, he has prospered in the client management side of the business. Because of his many qualities, Brian could be featured in several chapters of this book. He is in this chapter not only because he is creative, but because his many other skills work together to nurture creativity in a business that depends on new ideas to flourish.

Brian recognizes where his creativity comes from: "My creativity is an extension of humor. I think that a very active sense of humor is creativity. It's lateral thinking. It's taking some input and putting a spin on it; taking the obvious and making it insightfully funny." Brian's love of the movies, a medium with many similarities to television commercials, also keeps him in touch with both creative and production developments.

Brian came to Dailey as a trainee in 1981 with a well-developed sense of empathy, "I am blessed to have moved around a lot in my life. I have lived in the Midwest and in several other states. There is a genuineness there that is part of me. I feel I can relate to a housewife in Des Moines, Iowa, who shops in a supermarket. I feel I know that person." In fact, Brian lived in eight states growing up—Illinois, Iowa, Pennsylvania, Ohio, New York, Connecticut, Arizona, and California. This gave him an advantage, "I feel I know the consumer better than some people."

Brian graduated from Southern Methodist University in 1975 with a BA English, and went on to earn his master's degree in student personnel and counseling from Miami University in Ohio in 1977. After stints as assistant dean at SMU from 1977 to 1979, and as a salesperson for Equitable Life Assurance Company in Phoenix from 1979 to 1981, he joined on at Dailey.

Brian had a good feeling about Dailey right away because people there seemed to appreciate his leadership, humor, and creativity. He was gratified that his life experience up to this point helped train him for his job at Dailey.

"I realized that while I did not have specific advertising or business training when I joined Dailey, 90 percent of what was going to make me successful, I already had," says Brian. "I think a lot of that has to do with interpersonal communication skills, listening skills, and team work. I had a master's degree in counseling and became an assistant dean of students. This background made me good with clients and people because I listened to and heard what they were saying between the lines. I knew what people meant, not just what they said."

Brian's sense of humor, which fuels his creativity, also helps him as a manager. "A sense of humor can lighten things up when it is appropriate and loosen things up so people can be creative," says Brian. "I admit that most things are taken seriously. We need to have a proper perspective, and sometimes the right little zinger can do that." He adds, "I try with my humor to help people feel positive and like they are with a friend. It helps to make a human connection. That is my strength. Maybe once and a while I will say something smart in a meeting, but I am also trying to get the environment right for good results. That is an indication of my style as a consensus builder." His pastor, Gary Dennis, sees his humor from a different perspective: "He holds onto things very lightly. He has a wonderful sense of humor. He doesn't have to win every day, which probably lets him win far more times than the person who is driven to never lose a battle."

Brian's empathy, which helps his creativity, also helps him as a manager. "I never forget that I wasn't born a boss. I remember like it was yesterday that I was low man on the totem pole. I remember what was important to me—how important praise and recognition were, how important it was for someone to notice I was working late, and to know what I contributed to a project. I think I am good at recognizing and praising people at all levels. I remember that it was important for the boss to know my name. I remember how cool it was that the boss knew the name of everyone, including the cleaning staff at night."

Brian acts in big and small ways to let people know that he cares. Since Morris joined Dailey, Coke from the company machine has been reduced to a mere 25 cents. He returns every phone call he gets the same day or by noon the following day. He writes thank-you notes almost every day, "I thank people for the smallest to the biggest of achievements." He is not an e-mail kind of guy. Rather he gets out and visits people to know what the business and people pulse is. He adds, "I think we are a company with a heart. I like to think that I have something to do with that."

With these qualities, it is not surprising that people experience Brian as a positive and happy person. He recognizes that he is part cheerleader, and if he is down it affects others.

His primary motivation in life is clear: "I am driven by being a good person, a citizen of the Earth, more than I am to be a successful businessperson. This is going to sound naïve, but I have never seen a correlation between work and money. Money is a result of work, but I have not been driven by it. I am fortunate to be married to someone who does not expect that from me."

These qualities have led to great success at Dailey and to wide recognition that Brian is a truly nice guy, a label Brian values: "Some people view being nice as being wimpy. In my eyes, it translates to confidence, good self-esteem, and leadership." Phil Joanou describes Brian as having "a very calm leadership style. He is calm, but not weak; a very strong guy."

In 1996, the Western States Advertising Agencies recognized this when they named him Leader of the Year. The invitation to the dinner has a picture of Brian helping an elderly woman across the street.

Dennis notes Brian's broader life perspective, "He recognizes that life is so much bigger than being president of Dailey." Brian is deeply involved in his church and community, especially when it comes to helping those most in need of help. Brian and his wife Cindy have been married almost 30 years. Cindy is his guiding light—"She has a huge heart and is very kind," says Brian.

Cliff and Brian are a terrific team. They are excellent guiding lights for creativity and life. If someone wanted role models, these two would be an excellent place to start.

Concluding Thoughts

Cliff and Brian are the two examples in this book that I knew before I started the book. They led the agency where I used to develop advertising for Bartles & Jaymes. You may recall the humorous "Frank and Ed" campaign of the 1980s, a much-loved advertising campaign. Hal Riney originated the campaign, and Dailey and Associates became the agency a couple of years after its start.

Working with Cliff and Brian on humorous advertising was a thrill. While developing advertising, I reviewed about ten ads for every one we actually produced. As a result, I saw lots of highly creative, very funny work. We also had occasions of spontaneously creating a new ad while we were shooting an agreed-to ad. We would be on the set and see possibilities for something even better.

On one occasion, necessity became the mother of invention. The person who played Frank Bartles arrived on the set with a mild case of laryngitis—too much cheering at the Dodgers game the night before—making the planned ad impossible. While the actor went to a doctor to get the most out of his voice that day, the agency, including Cliff, set out to create a new ad that would take advantage of the actor's fading voice. They had a superb response—an ad where he admits his voice is going, and that the previously silent Ed would have to finish the ad, creating a stir at the news conference they find themselves in. Ed does finish the ad, but not by speaking. Instead, he holds up a sign with the similar tagline, "Thank You for Your Support."

Creativity is one of the most valuable skills any leader can have. It is something we are all capable of doing. That insight alone can open the flow of creativity in many people who assumed people had to be born creative. Creativity does not have to be a struggle. In fact, creativity is at its best when it flows effortlessly. Knowing this and knowing how to make it effortless opens the flow of creativity for many people.

Creativity is fun, even joyful when you are fully in the flow. It also is one of the most powerful activities a leader conducts. Powerful and fun—a wonderful combination.

Enjoy!

EPILOGUE

Thank you for reading this book.

You have gotten to know some fascinating people. I hope their examples inspire you to follow your path of wisdom.

The qualities leading to the path of wisdom fall into two groups: The first and largest group are the factors needed to create the foundation and environment for wisdom to emerge. For example, it is difficult for wisdom to emerge when trust is low between people in an organization. When trust is low, the focus is often on emotions (anxiety and fear) and logical thoughts (plotting and defending). With so much of our focus outwardly directed, it is difficult to have an awareness of our quiet, wise inner world. Our inner world is churning and chattering. For wisdom to emerge, a high degree of inner quiet and calmness must exist.

The other factors in the early chapters all contribute to creating an environment conducive to awakening the wisdom in all of us. Listening, sharing, and cooperation all build on each other. While they are all individually powerful, together they create an awesome power. The power translates into superior business results and people who are starting to realize their full abilities.

With a rising self-esteem and realization of their abilities, people in an organization quickly realize they are having fun. Fun is the turbo booster of a successful business. When people have fun, they optimize their skills and learn more than they ever have before.

At this point, life becomes more balanced. Each life role is nourished and eventually a whole life emerges.

All these qualities are positive ones. In fact, if there is a theme to this first group of qualities: We should strive to create a 100 percent positive environment, 100 percent of the time.

For some, this may sound naïve. For others, it may seem impossible and even undesirable. For just a few moments, I ask again that you put these preconceptions aside. The permission that you have to put these preconceptions aside comes from two of the wisest leaders we have seen. If Jesus had one message for us, it was that God is love. When we experience the power of love, we have no question about its paramount power. We can be in love with another person or with our vision of the future.

The other great leader with a very enduring message was the Buddha. He spoke of the power of compassion for others. In those moments (usually all to a few) when our hearts have gone out to another person, we've experienced the highly attractive power of compassion.

Love and compassion are highly compatible and synergistic.

If these two qualities are indeed the two most powerful in our world, then the goal of being 100 percent positive, 100 percent of the time appears to be on solid ground. Qualities such as trust, listening, and sharing start us along the road to creating that kind of environment. It is only when we get very good at building trust in an organization, listening with an open heart, and sharing to the fullest, that the dramatic power of a highly positive environment reveals itself.

With the foundation and environmental qualities in place, we are ready for wisdom to guide our actions. This leads to the second group of qualities, made up of the last three in the book.

A growing sense of spirit is a fascinating and joyous experience. It is happening to a growing number of people who encounter spirit by following a wide variety of paths. Some find spirit in the traditional religions, such as Christianity and Judaism. Others find spirit in Eastern wisdom traditions, like

Paramahansa Yogananda's Self-Realization Fellowship. And yet others find it in conversations with friends or by reading a book that somehow found them. The path also includes the many self-help and personal growth programs that develop a greater sense of self-awareness and motivate us to be kinder and more caring people.

Whatever the path, when encountered there is a deep sense of inner knowing that we are on the right path. For some there is a thrill of learning. For others, there is a deep sense of remembering what we have seem to have forgotten.

Intuition and creativity are strongly linked. Both qualities are very important business skills. These skills lead to a new way of managing and working. Win-win solutions and actions that help others become the norm, not the exception. "Thinking outside the box" also becomes the norm.

These qualities often lead to a manager redefining their role. Instead of being the director and main inventor of everything they are responsible for, they take on a very different role. They now see themselves as a facilitator, they see themselves as someone who helps others achieve what they want. For example, they unlock resources and use their experience to solve thorny questions. The difference is that they only provide help when it is asked for. They feel free to ask the question, "How can I help you today?" They respond with more of a sense of serving the other person than directing them.

Managers who are excellent facilitators have people working for them who display high levels of creativity, initiative, and excellence in their work. It truly is how you unlock the very best in what everyone has to contribute. The manager who is an excellent facilitator consistently achieves superior results.

Once recognized and in place, these qualities lead to a redefinition of success. No longer is material accumulation the only major measure. A broad view towards other qualities of life measures emerges and organizations use their vast and powerful resources increasingly to help others.

I hope this book has connected with your inner wisdom and inspired you to follow your unique path. The wonder of the path of wisdom is that while we have a deep personal inner sense of what is right, that inner sense is really a connection with the universal wisdom that guides all of us. Therein lies the magic that leads us to act with compassion in our hearts and with an inner guidance system that leads to the path of least resistance.

Enjoy! Namaste.

Recommended Reading

Bailey, Alice. *A Treatise on White Magic.* New York: Lucis Publishing Co., 1951.

This is one of 24 volumes of the Ageless Wisdom brought to us by Alice Bailey through the assistance of a great Tibetan master, Djwhal Khul. This is not easy reading, but if you select one volume to start with it may be the right one for you.

Blanchard, Ken, and Michael O'Conner. *Managing by Values.* San Francisco: Berrett-Koehler, 1997.

Ken is the author of the *One Minute Manager,* which is insightful and easy reading like this book. Knowing an organization's values and managing by them is becoming increasingly important.

Case, Jack. *The Open-Book Experience.* Reading, Mass.: Addison-Wesley, 1998.

Open-book management is a wonderful way to increase trust and dramatically improve results. Jack Case shares the lessons and successes of over 100 companies in this easy-reading book.

Chopra, Deepak. *The Seven Spiritual Laws of Success.* San Rafael, Calif.: Amber-Allen Publishing, 1995.

This is one of the most successful and popular overtly spiritual books in the last ten years. As a Western-trained physician, Chopra is a very credible spokesperson for Eastern wisdom in America. This book is easy, yet powerful reading.

Covey, Stephen R. *The Seven Habits of Highly Effective People.* New York: Fireside Books, 1990.

> This is one of the best-selling books of the 1990s. Its popularity comes from the simple, yet powerful advice that resonates deeply in most readers. There is a subtle spiritual thread that runs throughout this book. If you have not read it, it should be on your reading list.

Covey, Stephen R., A. Roger Merrill, and Rebecca R. Merrill. *First Things First.* New York: Simon and Schuster, 1994.

> This book takes one of Covey's seven habits and expands it into a full book. One of the biggest insights many business people take away from this book is that they are not spending enough time on things that are important yet not urgent. They find that they are adrenaline-junkies who focus too much on today.

The Dalai Lama. *The Good Heart.* Boston: Wisdom Publications, 1998.

> The Dalai Lama is one of the most inspiring people on our planet now. In this book, he discusses Buddhism and Christianity and underscores the similarities in the messages from Buddha and Jesus.

Dyer, Wayne W. *Manifest Your Destiny.* New York: HarperCollins, 1998.

> This is an amazing book for anyone with a background in Western psychology. It is probably unlike any other book on the subject that you have ever read. The advice in this book has a distinctly Eastern and spiritual flavor. It's powerful advice will be difficult for many people to assimilate on their first reading.

———. *Wisdom of the Ages.* New York: HarperCollins, 1998.

> Dyer presents the thinking of the major thinkers of the last few centuries in an easy-reading book. From Confucius to Mother Teresa he covers the eternal truths we all live by.

Fritz, Robert. *The Path of Least Resistance.* Salem, Mass.: Fawcett Books, 1989.

This book is more than 20 years old, but it is still one of the most powerful books about creativity that you can buy. Fritz was a classically trained musician who wondered how creativity happened. His insights are some of the clearest available to us today.

Fukuyama, Francis. *Trust.* New York: Simon & Schuster, 1995.

This well-documented book details the important role trust plays in economics and culture. It's a fascinating book that was a bestseller in its time.

Hemsath, Dave, and Leslie Yerkes. *301 Ways to Have Fun at Work.* San Francisco: Berrett-Koehler, 1997.

Having fun enriches life and actually improves results and productivity at work. This book provides suggestions that all of us can adapt to our situations.

Jones, Susan Smith. *Choose to Live Peacefully.* Berkeley, Calif.: Celestial Arts, 1991.

Jones has several books with similar titles, and each of them is easy reading that can make practical changes to your life.

Keyes, Ken Jr. *Handbook to Higher Consciousness.* Coos Bay, Ore.: Love Line Books, 1989.

This was a popular book in the 1980s because it clearly articulated levels of consciousness most of us go through. This oft-quoted book is easy, powerful reading.

Leonard, Thomas J., with Byron Laursen. *The Portable Coach.* New York: Scribners, 1998.

Thomas is seen by many as the founder of personal coaching. He founded Coach University and continues to be the profession's leading thinker. This book does a wonderful job of bringing personal coaching to life.

Lynn, Adele B. *In Search of Honor.* Belle Vernon, Penn.: Bajon House, 1998.

The author takes a very inspiring approach to building trust in life. She provides excellent practical advice all managers can use.

Ornish, Dean. *Love and Survival.* New York: HarperCollins, 1999.

You know that love is powerful, but you probably never guessed it was this powerful. The author uses scientific studies to underscore love's power.

Pedler, Mike, John Burgoyne, and Tom Boydell. *The Learning Company.* New York: McGraw-Hill, 1997.

These authors take a very different approach to the learning company concept, at least as articulated by Senge in *The Fifth Discipline.* They have plenty of practical advice and examples.

Robbins, Anthony. *Personal Power II* (book, cassette, video edition). San Diego, Calif.: Nightingale-Conant Corp., 1996.

This may be the best-selling tape series of the last decade. If you follow Robbins's advice, you will make very positive changes in your life.

Roman, Sanaya. *Living with Joy.* Tiburon, Calif.: H. J. Kramer, 1986.

Easy and fun reading is a good way to characterize this book. The fun comes from powerful insights about our universe that are presented in a thoroughly understandable manner. This book changed my life.

Rosenbluth, Hal F., and Diane McFerrin Peters. *The Customer Comes Second.* New York: William Morrow, 1992.

Hal transformed a sleepy, regional company into a dynamic international company by making employees number one. His book is filled with wonderful examples that inspire many managers to follow his path.

Schucman, Helen. *A Course in Miracles*. Tiburon, Calif.: Foundation for Inner Peace, 1996.

This is a wonderful book that, if read and studied every day for a year, will contribute to making some of the most positive changes in your life. The messages in this book come from an inspired and wise source.

Senge, Peter M. *The Fifth Discipline*. New York: Doubleday, 1990.

This is a bestseller that defined for some people the concept of a learning company. Senge offers powerful insight into the systemic nature of a company's problems and how they are rooted in often-hidden internal values and beliefs.

Sogyal Rinpoche. *The Tibetan Book of Living and Dying*. San Francisco: HarperSanFrancisco, 1992.

Next to the Dalai Lama, Sogyal Rinpoche may be the most articulate teacher of Buddhism in the West today. When I studied with him, I learned how compassionate, wise, and joyful a human being can be.

Swami Rama. *The Art of Joyful Living*. Honesdale, Penn.: The Himalayan Institute Press, 1989.

This is one of the more descriptive and accurate titles I've seen for a book. Swami Rama is a revered Indian spiritual teacher.

Templeton, John Marks. *From the Worldwide Laws of Life*. Philadelphia: Templeton Foundation Press, 1997.

The author is the founder of highly successful Templeton mutual funds. After retiring from this business, he dedicated himself to writing about spirituality, especially how spirituality and science connect. This is a wonderful book that may be one of the easiest to read on a subject that can be complex.

Vaughan, Frances; Walsh, Roger, editors; Mack, John. *Paths Beyond Ego, The Transpersonal Vision (A New Consciousness Reader)*. New York: J. P. Tarcher, 1993.

This anthology outlines what is one of the most interesting developments in psychology in the last couple decades. A variety of writers, including Ken Wilber, make for very powerful reading.

Walsch, Neale Donald. *Conversations with God, Book 1.* Charlottesville, Va.: Putnam Publishing Group, 1996.

———. *Conversations with God, Books 2 and 3.* Charlottesville, Va.: Hampton Roads, 1997, 1998.

This is an intriguing series of books. If you put aside the question of whether these books record actual conversations with God, this series offers some very practical insights and interesting reading.

Wilber, Ken. *No Boundary.* Boston: Shambhala, 1979.

As one of the founders of transpersonal psychology, Ken Wilber has helped connect the Western science of psychology with Eastern wisdom traditions.

Yogananda, Paramahansa. *Autobiography of a Yogi.* Los Angeles: Self-Realization Fellowship, 1994.

The founder of the Self Realization Fellowship Yogananda has left us with practical lessons for daily living that are among the most transforming I am aware of. He is one of the foremost spiritual teachers in this century, in my opinion.

Zukav, Gary. *Seat of the Soul.* New York: Fireside Books, 1990.

If you want to understand what the soul really is, this is must reading for you. His book has been around for some time and recently received a big boost in popularity through his appearance on *Oprah.* Zukav has the ability to explain the soul in terms that most everyone can understand.

INDEX